To Jeff:

The best of success in all your Alaska fishing adventures.

Christopher Batin

4/4/91

CHRIS BATIN'S 20 GREAT

Alaska Fishing

Adventures

CHRIS BATIN'S 20 GREAT

Alaska Fishing Adventures

by Christopher Batin

Foreword by Jack Brown
Photographs by Christopher and Adela Batin
Illustrations by Jeff Schuler

Published by Alaska Angler Publications
Fairbanks, Alaska

Chris Batin's 20 Great Alaska Fishing Adventures is part of the Alaska Angling and Hunting LibraryTM, which is dedicated to providing only the very finest in Alaska hunting and fishing literature.

Published by Alaska Angler Publications, P. O. Box 83550, Fairbanks, Alaska 99708, (907) 456-8212.

First Edition, March 1991

Book and cover design: Adela Ward Batin
Typography and production: Award Design, Fairbanks, Alaska
Maps and illustrations: Jeff Schuler
Photography: Christopher and Adela Batin

Library of Congress Cataloging in Publication Data
Batin, Christopher—
    Chris Batin's 20 Great Alaska Fishing Adventures: a travel planning guide for those who want the best in Alaska sportfishing.

        1. Fishing—Alaska.

SH467.B38   1991

Library of Congress Card Catalog Number: 90-084906

ISBN 0-916771-09-1 (Trade Edition)

Produced in the State of Alaska
Printed in the United States of America

The Kenai: River of Trophy Kings and Tikchik Char Extravaganza by Chris Batin originally appeared in Petersen's FISHING and have been reprinted with permission of Petersen's FISHING.

Dedication

To my grandparents and great grandparents:
Pauline Whitlock, Rose Batin, William Batin,
Eva Szabo, Frank Rosati Sr., and Rose Rosati.

Your personal stories of overcoming unbelievable odds
and hardships have been an inspiration and strength in my life.

And to the memory of Nick Jennings,
a fishing guide whose love for Alaska's wilderness northcountry
was only surpassed by his reverence for the God who created it.

Author's note

*In our extensive fishing adventures throughout the state, Adela and I
adhere to a strict catch and release policy, taking only those fish that are
mortally wounded, or a few salmon we wish to keep for our own
personal use. Of the 75 fish that appear in this book, 14 (excluding
marine species that were gaffed or caught on bait) had to be dispatched
due to bleeding, hook injury, shock or other factors. When you consider
the hundreds of sportfish we've caught while experiencing these 20
adventures, the final figure is a fraction of a percent.*

*It's a fact of life that sportfishing and some percentage of mortality go
hand in hand, no matter how careful the angler or the methods used. If
a fish had to be dispatched, or was caught by an angler for mounting,
we made the most of it and photographed the fish in a number of ways
that would have been impractical to accomplish on live fish.*

*This in no way implies a "keep everything you catch" philosophy on
our part, but rather, a personal obligation—as educators of Alaska
sportfishing—to share the beauty of these sportfish with you, and also the
sadness when one is lost. Intentional killing for vanity's sake is so final
and passe'. It's our hope that when you do have the option to keep or
release a fish, that you choose the latter whenever possible.*

*By practicing catch and release we encourage the continuance of this
renewable resource and give future generations the opportunity to enjoy
the special joys of sportfishing in Alaska.—CMB*

Table of Contents

Adventure 1   Expedition to Aniakchak   14

Adventure 2   Susitna's King of the Flies   24

Adventure 3   Naknek's October Rainbows   34

Adventure 4   Tikchik Char Extravaganza   44

Adventure 5   American Wellesley Pike   56

Adventure 6   Beaver Creek Grayling   64

Adventure 7   The Kenai: River of Trophy Kings   74

Adventure 8   Fishing in the Land of Midnight Fire   86

Adventure 9   The Allure of Iliamna   94

Adventure 10   Make a Date with a Shee   106

Adventure 11   World-Class Fishing Indulgence
               at Bristol Bay   118

Adventure 12   Flat Island Flatfish   130

Adventure 13   Talkeetna's Rainbow Splendor   140

Adventure 14   Fishing the Aniak: An Adventure
               for the Strong of Heart   150

Adventure 15   Grand Slam Salmon of
               Southwest Alaska   156

Adventure 16   Cook Inlet's King of Kings   166

Adventure 17   Admiralty Island: Gateway
               to Angling Adventure   174

Adventure 18   Fishing Alaska's Last Great Wilderness:
               The Arctic National Wildlife Refuge   182

Adventure 19   The Challenging Chinooks of
               Alaska's Chuit River   192

Adventure 20   Tongass Trout and Salmon
               on a Budget   200

               Free Information for
               Planning Your Trip   208

               About the Author   210

Foreword

FOR MANY OF US WHO LIVE AND LABOR IN THE LOWER 48 STATES, Alaska holds out the promise of adventure, excitement and visual splendor. We may be cooped up in a smoky city, or stuck with the sameness of fishing in the local pond. 'Way up north, though, exists a land where rivers run red with giant salmon, great halibut prowl in glacier-bound fjords, and trout grow to be stupendous in mighty wilderness streams.

As "America's Last Frontier," Alaska occupies a special place in the minds of Americans. Where else in the U.S. does the sun merely touch the horizon during 24 hours of a summer day? Who can imagine living through a winter where the brightest daytime light comes from the aurora borealis? Where the flowers and grasses of the snow-free months are underlain by permanently frozen ground, and rivers spring full-strength from ancient ice?

The entire state thus speaks of adventure. And, it takes a special kind of writer to bring the Alaska adventure into perspective. Christopher Batin has accomplished that feat with this book.

Although he is Alaskan through and through, Chris hardly matches the popular conception of a burly, tough-talking "sourdough." For that matter, he looks as though he would be more at home selling real estate in Cincinnati. Chris' quick smile and modulated voice belie the truth that he fly fishes for stupendous salmon, cheats death while floating raging rivers, flies with bush pilots into the face of horrible weather, and otherwise does what comes with the job of being an outdoor journalist and fishing writer in Alaska.

Batin and I were thrown together in 1982 after the publisher of my magazine asked the publisher of the magazine for whom Chris then worked to recommend an Alaska outdoor writer. That publisher (possibly with malice aforethought) suggested his own editor. I wrote to Chris, outlining our needs, and he replied with something less than enthusiasm. "I write in a moody style that our Alaskan readers seem to prefer, and I don't think your readers will appreciate it," he said. "Besides," he added, "I prefer to write for magazines that pay a great deal more than you do."

Batin immediately became a challenge—although I believe my actual reaction was, "Cheeky S.O.B.—I'll teach him!"

We taught each other, though, during the ongoing course of a writer/editor relationship that quickly broadened into friendship.

And through this friendship with Chris, I learned about Alaska—particularly fishing in Alaska.

Through his writings, I experienced the sensation of floating a roaring, treacherous river on the Alaska Peninsula. I have gripped my chair arms, imagining a white-knuckle flight into a craggy wilderness of the Brooks Range. With Chris Batin's descriptions to guide me, I have caught the elusive and mysterious sheefish of the Far North and wrestled with the giant halibut of Southeast Alaska. King salmon and steelhead, arctic char and grayling, silvers and chums, cutthroat and Dolly Varden, pike and heavy rainbow trout, have leaped and struggled and fought in my mind, thanks to the words placed on paper by Chris Batin.

After these years of receiving and editing fishing stories from Chris, I thought I knew all there was to know about angling in the 49th State. But I was wrong. For you see, I was privileged to edit this book, and thus was given a fullscale advanced education in the adventures of fishing in Alaska.

The pleasure of fishing isn't the end of the experience in Alaska, however. After all, the worst fishing in Alaska beats the best fishing in the Lower 48. Perhaps local anglers in Montana, Wyoming, Colorado, Idaho and such places will argue with that statement, but most will concede that the experience of Alaska can't be equalled.

For flat-out, incredible adventure in fishing, there's Alaska. All else pales in comparison with The Last Frontier. And, if anybody can capture the spirit of that adventure, it's Christopher Batin. Now, let's settle back and enjoy through this book the excitement of fishing in Christopher Batin's magnificent Alaska.

Jack Brown, Editor
Western Outdoors
Costa Mesa, California

Author Chris Batin exploring the crystal-clear waters of Lake Beverley located in the Wood River-Tikchik area.

Introduction

CHOOSING GREAT ALASKA SPORTFISHING ADVENTURES is like being a kid in a candy store: the selection is often too large and varied to single out an all-time favorite.

I faced a similar dilemma in choosing my favorite fishing adventures for this book. Like a kid with eyes widened with anticipation, I easily fell into temptation and succumbed to no less than 20 choices, with eyes still hungry for more. But I make no apologies.

Veteran anglers know that each Alaska fishing adventure appeals to a specific sweet tooth or hankering. The adventure that is ultimately chosen depends on many factors: a few of these include time of day, mood and finances of the fisherman. For some, a trip to the Kenai is world-class excitement, while others require Bristol Bay and more elite methods of fishing to enjoy the same euphoria.

Whatever adventure is chosen, whether it be roadside fishery or remote fly-in, remember that half the fun of searching for Alaska's great fisheries comes from sampling the different waters, areas and species.

And there's much to sample. If it's power fishing you want, choose fly fishing for 40-pound-plus king salmon on small clear-water streams out of Talkeetna. The finesse and stress-relieving qualities of dry fly fishing for grayling and char in the Arctic National Wildlife Refuge can't be beat. And if you're still not satisfied, fly to the far end of the Alaska Peninsula and tie into headstrong silvers in all their raw, untamed fury.

The material for this book was not gathered from the comforts of an easy chair. For nearly two decades, I've spent up to 180 days a year fishing throughout the state, experiencing the best...and worst...of Alaska sportfishing. Because the Alaska sportfishing I knew years ago is fast disappearing, I've picked 20 adventures that you can experience now, in all their grandeur, before they, too, disappear with the passage of time and increased angling pressure.

In the meantime, I'll be writing up the many other adventures I have not listed. These include floating mouse patterns for husky rainbow trout on Kodiak Island, fishing for steelhead in the Sitkoh Creek area rainforests, or dry fly fishing for world-record grayling out of Nome. At another time, in another book, we'll discover these and other fisheries. But like that kid in a candy store, it's best to enjoy and savor the first selections, then move on to others.

When reading this book, take time to study the photographs. I offer them not as proof of each adventure, but rather, as visual enhancements to show what's waiting for you.

Of course, expect each chapter to offer specific information on the best flies, lures and techniques to use for each adventure. Do not use these fish-catching secrets to rape a watershed of its prized possessions, but rather, to experience and enjoy each fishery to its fullest.

There is plenty to enjoy. Alaska is fishing's modern day Garden of Eden. Each mountain, stream and fish is charged with the power of the Almighty. And anglers are the stewards of this garden's splendor, to harvest and sample its wares, to oversee and protect it, and to love it. It's a responsibility many anglers—residents and non-residents alike—need to take seriously.

One more word of advice. After reading each adventure in this book, occasionally pause for a moment and close your eyes. Toss aside the macho angler image, and open up the ears to your soul. Each area has its own personality, its own language. When you feel the land or a particular fish pull a heartstring or two, don't resist. Each has much to say.

Through the pages of this book, let's become good friends and share, as friends do, our time together, exploring the thrills and wonders of Alaska's finest sport fishing opportunities. Now if you're ready, I hear the winds of Aniakchak calling us to adventure in Chapter 1.

Christopher Batin
Fairbanks, Alaska

1 Adventure

An angler fishing a stream along the rugged coastline of the Alaska Peninsula, east of Aniakchak.

Expedition to Aniakchak

ANIAKCHAK is an experience that anglers seldom boast about openly, and for good reason. Many have trouble finding words to describe it, while others find themselves in mental solitude, coping with soul-jarring images before those first words finally break free. Often, in the process of remembering, a drop of sweat forms above the brow, an arm muscle twitches in response to a frightful moment, or a smile forms to a generic image of fish and angler, a symbolic reminder of the hundreds of fish that were caught and released.

Each trip has the same basic elements: the journey, the fish, and the ever-present volcanic crater that covers 30 square miles, with a six-mile-wide core. Dark and foreboding structures—lava flows, ominous cinder cones and explosion pits—resemble medieval gargoyles rimming the brow of the volcanic caldera. Winds rising up from the Gulf of Alaska buffet a knobby backbone of mountains, scouring the slopes clean of any plant life. When viewed separately, these elements are pieces to a puzzle that have no rhyme or reason. Yet when fitted together they form the picture of Aniakchak, one of the last great wilderness fishing adventures in North America.

The bald eagle, Nature's master aviator, is one of the few birds that can handle the 60-plus miles-per-hour turbulence above Aniakchak's mountains. The eagle that Bob Graham observed from afar early one September morning rode the ripping torrents of air masterfully in Peanut Butter Pass, an isolated, volcanic valley with an alpine so foreboding that the the gulls, hawks and ravens keep to the safety of the lowland forests.

Suddenly, the eagle folded its wings and rolled 360 degrees in a sudden updraft. Its head darted quickly back and forth, as if shocked at the sight of the Cessna 180 as it whined past at over 140 mph.

"Don't believe that eagle knew what to make of us," Graham said, in a touch of amazement. The two anglers craned their necks to view the rapidly disappearing bird. But their view was cut short. Without warning, a down draft sledgehammered the plane 100 feet into a swirling nightmare of turbulence. Gravity disappeared and gear ricocheted off the cabin walls. The back seat separated from its latches, slamming the two passengers head first into the cabin ceiling and the fishing rods that stretched down the middle.

"Hold on," Graham said, "we're in for a rough ride."

Smiles and jokes about the upcoming fishing extravaganza ceased immediately. The anglers' knuckles, rimmed in white, grasped the underside of the airplane seats. Graham slowly shook his head as the plane buffeted in the turbulence.

"That sucker hole ahead is closing up real fast," he said, referring to a bright, sunlit opening in the clouds at the end of the

Guide Jon Kent caught this Dolly Varden char while dead drifting an egg pattern. During August and September, it's common to catch 50 to 100 char per day. Fly rods, barbless flies and a catch and release philosophy are prerequisites for all participants.

2,000-foot boxed canyon.

We saw the sucker hole as a hypnotic eye, daring us to take the chance to cross over into what one client called, "The Land of Plenty Fish." Yet conditions quickly worsened. Flashes of mountain peaks, their crowns potmarked by past volcanic and glacial activity, reached out to grab our wingtips. Nearing the sucker hole, glimpses of vertical rock cliffs broke through the layer of clouds.

"Just a bit more elevation..."

Looking down into the sucker hole, there was a vortex of white clouds, with no bottom to be seen. "No can do," Graham said. "Hold on."

It was a combination of elements that could have sent many lesser pilots to their death. Rather than making a wide circle, and risking the chance of a down draft shooting the plane into the ground, Graham tilted the Cessna on its side, and let it drop. The stall buzzer came on. With the force of a spiked volleyball, we shot nearly 1,000 feet to earth.

At about 600 feet, Graham righted the plane, rode an updraft for about 200 feet, and tracked to the center of the valley.

"There's usually an up draft at the bottom of these down drafts," he said in as comforting a tone as possible to the wide-eyed passengers. "No matter. The fish will still be there this afternoon. We'll give it a try again, once the clouds open up."

Four hours later, Graham was gratified to see the anglers waiting at the plane a few minutes prior to departure.

What could possibly convince anglers to place their lives in the hands of bush pilots who push their skills to the max in a wilderness arena where a single mistake could result in a fireball on some unexplored mountainside? Surely the element of the unknown in such a unique environment is a factor. But there's another part that supersedes the awesome magnetism of this volcanic wasteland. Through the roaring wind of Aniakchak, anglers hear a siren's song from nearby streams and oceans that tugs at their souls and makes nerve endings alive with tingly excitement. For there they discover September's Big Three: char, rainbow trout, and silver salmon, living threads that weave an intricate tapestry of Alaska sport-fishing adventure.

Guide Jon Kent knows the allure of the Big Three in the Aniakchak area. While waiting for the weather to lift one after-noon, he walked the banks of a major river, searching for a suitable lunch spot. He picked up pieces of driftwood strewn amid 15-inch brown bear tracks pressed deeply into patches of mud. At river's edge, guest Richard Kaplan hooked a nice silver salmon on his first cast of the day, landed it and donated it for lunch. It was the focal point of conversation in describing this fall fishery.

"Salmon are the key that makes for such a fishing extravaganza this time of year," Kent said. "If you think it's rough getting here, you should see what the fish have to go through."

He said that during the summer, schools of char and rainbows are dispersed in lakes and deep rivers in nearby watersheds.

"Anglers who fish Alaska during the traditional peak fishing months of June and July don't experience this type of fishing ac-tion," Kent said. "The char and bows are too spread out and hard to reach. However, in late summer, sockeye salmon are the

biological magnets that draw these species out of their deepwater haunts."

And what a magnet. According to biologists, a single sockeye hen averages about 3,000 eggs. Multiply this by the millions of sockeye entering Bristol Bay area streams to spawn each year, and you have an idea as to the magnitude, and importance, of this fishery. But the sockeyes are just a preview of action to come.

"In early September, the sockeyes start dying off and the silvers enter the same watersheds," Kent said. "Silvers in this area are powerful and chrome-bright from the ocean, run from eight to 20 pounds, and very aggressive. The char and rainbows run anywhere from two to five pounds, with some going as high as 10."

Nearby, Kaplan quickly hooked and fought a char. It tail-spinned on the river's surface, jumped once and broke off. Kaplan shrugged and tied on another lure. The wind increased in force and created a chop at the river's mouth.

I reflected on what I knew of the area. "As strong as this fishery appears," I said, "it's really a fragile giant. The char and rainbows expose themselves to predators, disease and injury by migrating into these shallow spawning streams to feed on salmon eggs. If they don't, the alternative is death through starvation. Salmon eggs enhance the rainbows' and chars' chances of overwinter survival, as the fish face a six to eight-month period when the lakes and streams are at least partially covered with ice, making for adverse feeding conditions. Nutrient-rich salmon eggs provide the fat necessary for the fish to survive the winter. It isn't a selective thing, either. It seems every char in the watershed is feeding on salmon eggs, 24 hours a day."

Silver salmon start entering Peninsula streams the last week in August. The area's cloudy, inclement weather often requires salmon anglers to use fluorescent flies and lures for best success.

Kaplan hooked a spunky silver that threw a fountain of spray with the first hookset.

"Silver salmon also contribute to the scene," I continued. "After they spawn and die, nutrients released from the decaying carcasses stimulate primary production for next year's invertebrate populations, which both salmon fry, char and trout feed upon. The result is superior fishing opportunities that don't know when to quit. Indeed, the Aniakchak area offers some of the best sportfishing I've experienced in Alaska."

According to a scant few biological surveys conducted in the area, streams near Aniakchak contain mostly char, Dolly Varden, silver and red salmon, while those to the north and west host additional populations of rainbow trout. The "Big Three" can be caught with a few basic techniques.

For char, Kent likes to dead drift salmon egg patterns through holes and along riffles, right behind migrating or holding salmon.

"You can see the salmon from shore," he said. "Fish around them. Char and rainbow are feeding so aggressively that they often nail a bright orange strike indicator, or you'll see the wake of five char following a Glo-Bug as you skitter it across the surface. Because they feed strictly on eggs, they can be very finicky. It's good to have several colors and sizes in your fly box."

Kent said fishing is good for as long as you can last. On one float, an angler caught 48 char in one morning, before breakfast. (Later on, I would personally catch 87 char in a single afternoon, all on a six-weight fly rod. I opted not to fish for char anymore that week, to minimize hooking mortality).

But the hero of the show is Aniakchak's silver salmon. They are

chunky, muscular fish that migrate into clear-water rivers and streams by the hundreds. Intertidal streams, where anglers catch fish on an incoming tide, are the most popular. Washington State angler Will Tinnesand was visibly impressed with the quality of the wilderness silver fishing.

"The fish enter streams in large schools," Tinnesand said, "hundreds of them at a time. And you are right there, watching them come in on the tide. They flash in the water like silver dollars. And boy, are they strong! Heck, to hook a fish, all it took was a cast, a two-handed hookset to bury the barb, and the fight was on. I landed 23 in a single afternoon, and missed about that many due to hook throws or missed strikes."

Tinnesand said he has fished for salmon throughout Alaska and the Northwest, and the Aniakchak area is the best he has seen.

"In some areas, you land on a wilderness beach, where the stream empties into the ocean," he said. "Other areas you fish upstream a ways. In one stream, I landed sockeye, char, chum and silvers all from one spot. I sure could have done without a few of those turbulent flights around Aniakchak. That's an experience in itself, but the fishing was worth it."

Indeed, reaching these prime fishing areas is a challenge, especially for the pilots.

"Landing strips, as most people know them, don't exist out here," said bush pilot Joe Maxey. "We utilize everything from volcanic cinder flats, narrow gravel bars to stretches of ocean beach."

He said there's always danger when flying in Aniakchak's remote areas and severe weather conditions. "Oftentimes pockets of soft

Adela Batin examines a whale skull found on a remote beach on the Alaska Peninsula. Japanese glass fishing floats, pieces of ship wreckage and myriad sea shells are oftentimes found by anglers who devote time to beachcombing.

sand can grab the plane's tires and tip it forward, crashing the plane. Or an ocean breaker can come in, grab a wheel, and tip the wing into the water, resulting in a destroyed airplane."

Maxey, an accomplished bush pilot, said despite the adverse conditions, he has yet to suffer a major accident. "I try to use caution, and don't take any unnecessary chances," he said.

Winds present the most danger, as we were to find out later that week. After a spectacular day of silver salmon fishing, Maxey tried taking off into a strong wind from a sandbar on the lower Alaska Peninsula. As we cleared the ground, a side gust hammered our plane sideways over a bunch of beach grass. The plane jerked sideways, and Maxey immediately landed the plane. A stump hidden in the grass had sheared off the plane's rear wheel. For three days we were stranded at the base camp on the stream, waiting for another plane to rescue us.

We told the others back in camp that we would be out fishing various streams for a couple of days, so they didn't come looking for us right away. We had nothing to do but fish for salmon. The stream was packed with silvers that year, and the four of us caught and released fish from daylight to dark. In a way, we were happy a plane came looking for us the third day. I don't know if we could have taken any more fish catchin'.

So, the next time you're taking a long, leisurely boat ride to your local fishing grounds, stop and remember those few lucky anglers riding the roller coaster turbulence over Aniakchak's coastal mountains. But don't think too hard about all the fish they'll be catching once they land. If the siren song gets to you like it did me, at least wait until your boat returns to the dock before joining them. It's a long swim to Alaska.

Planning Your Trip

ABOUT THE AREA

Aniakchak National Monument is home to the Aniakchak Caldera, created by the collapse of the central part of the volcano sometime after the last glaciation. Later activity built a cone, Vent Mountain, inside the caldera. Aniakchak last erupted in 1931. The caldera's Surprise Lake, which is heated by hot springs, tumbles out a 1,500-foot rift in the crater wall, and offers spectacular exploration when weather allows.

Area wildlife includes ptarmigan, caribou, brown bear and eagles. Sockeye salmon spawn in the Aniakchak River, which originates in Surprise Lake. Meat of fish from this river is recognizable by the flavor of soda and iron dissolved in the mineral-laden outflow.

While Aniakchak offers the best wilderness adventure, September's Big Three can be found in other areas and watersheds north of the region. Char and salmon can be caught in the streams south of the city of King Salmon that empty into either the Bering Sea or the Gulf of Alaska. Rainbows inhabit a few Peninsula streams, but are most abundant in the King Salmon and Becharof watersheds, and west into the Togiak and Nushagak river systems. Silvers and char are also extremely plentiful in these drainages.

WHEN TO GO

The last of August through the first week in September offers the best fishing for all four species of salmon, Dolly Varden and arctic char and, to the north, rainbow trout. The fishing for all but silver salmon gradually tapers off to season's end in mid October.

WHAT TO TAKE

Fly rodders should take a 5 or 6-weight rod, sink-tip line and floating line for trout and char, and an 8-weight for salmon. Best rainbow patterns have been egg-sucking leeches, zonkers and black marabou muddlers. Glo-Bug patterns in peach, pink and red are also very effective, followed by smolt and various nymph patterns. My favorite silver flies are Animated Alevin, Crinkle Hair Special, Baker Buster and Las Vegas Showgirl.

Spin fishermen do well with single-hook Pro-Guide spinners, Storm Wiggle Warts, Gibbs Koho and Kit-i-Mat spoons, as well as drifting Corkies and Spin N Glos.

HOW TO GET THERE

According to the National Park Service, Aniakchak is one of Alaska's most remote national monuments/preserves, and local weather can be severe at all seasons. Access is only by air. Take scheduled commercial air service from Anchorage to either King Salmon or Port Heiden. There you'll charter an air taxi to your drop-off location. Lodge operators generally schedule their pick-ups and departures from King Salmon.

WHERE TO STAY

Because of the severity of weather in the Aniakchak area, as well as a healthy brown bear population, only the most experienced wilderness campers should try a do-it-yourself trip. Several lodges offer full accommodations, as well as spike camps, throughout the area.

APPROXIMATE COST

Lodge and outpost camp operators offer food, shelter and air service to the best streams for $2,000 to $4,000 per week. Do-it-yourself charters depend on type of aircraft and flying time, averaging $250 an hour. Figure from $500 to $1,200 round trip from King Salmon to the major watersheds in the area.

WHO TO CONTACT

For a listing of guides, outfitters and do-it-yourself services, turn to page 208, "Free Information To Plan Your Trip."

2 Adventure

A fly-caught king in the glacially-turbid Talkeetna River. A stout 10-weight rod is required to handle large flies and big fish in strong current.

Susitna's King of the Flies

THE CONTEST WAS A MISMATCH FROM THE START.

The underdog was Rick Sanchez, a man in pursuit of a simple quest: to experience a good Alaska fly fishing experience with a reasonable chance of success. He wanted to catch king salmon on a fly. A handful would suffice; 10 or 15 in a week's time would be more than he dreamed possible.

In searching out his goal, Sanchez investigated Alaska's most publicized king salmon fisheries. He considered the Kenai, where unguided anglers catch an average of one king for every two to three days of fishing. The world-renown Nushagak was a possibility, yet its big-water nature, muddy currents and heavy fishing pressure detracted from the overall experience he craved.

Sanchez's caution was justified. For two years in a row, he suffered through less than desirable experiences at Alaska fishing lodges. He was nearly convinced that Alaska fishing was not all it was cracked up to be. This would be his last hurrah.

Rather than choosing a major king water, he decided on a small stream fishery in the Susitna drainage, one away from the crowds and seldom discussed in fly fishing circles.

Following the course of the glacial-fed Susitna River north out of

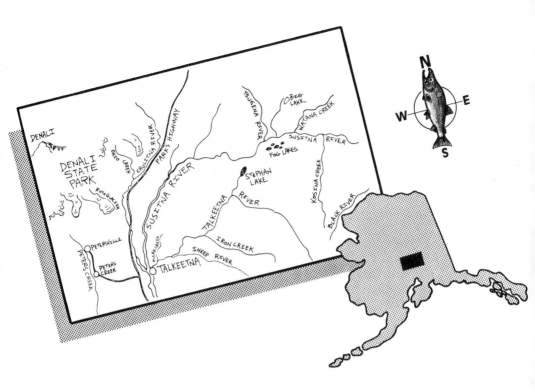

Anchorage, guide Jim Bailey flew Sanchez beyond the Chugach Range and into the wilds of the Talkeetna Mountains. Bailey banked the float plane sharply and pointed out several small tributaries Sanchez was to fish. The obstacles were complex and many.

About every 200 yards, one or more brown bears splashed through the shallows in pursuit of king and sockeye salmon. The hike from the drop-off point to the stream was anything but a leisurely stroll; it was a two-mile hike via moose and caribou trail. There was no word on fishing conditions; Sanchez was the first fly fisher on the stream that year. To complicate matters, the banks were thickly overgrown with brush and trees, which excluded everything except roll casts. The prognosis was not good.

All things considered, it was apparent that Rick Sanchez was destined to fail. The fact that he didn't is the crux of what angling accomplishments are made of.

By the time Sanchez stepped into the water's edge several hours later, his trepidation had changed to euphoria. In the clearwater stream, which was a mere 20 yards wide and four feet deep, were the oblong shapes of boulder-sized salmon. Some were finning lazily in the current. Others were vicious and territorial, snapping at smaller 30-pound kings for invading their space. The question remained: Would the fish take a fly?

Sanchez made his first cast. A quick twitch sank the fly into view of the salmon. He swam it through the current edge, mended his line and twitched it again.

A hook-kyped male cut a sizable wake in the water toward the fly. Sanchez twitched the fly to further irritate the fish. The 13-inch wide-tail swirled the current, shooting the 54-inch fish forward. Sanchez watched in wide-eyed amazement. The now seemingly miniscule 1/0 fly met its destiny as toothy, black-rimmed jaws chomped down on the orange and pink pattern.

The 10-weight rod was immediately humbled at the hookset, its stiff spine quivering in spasmodic undulations. In the clearwater stream, Sanchez watched the king shoot up the main channel, nearly colliding with a snag before turning and stripping another 75 yards of line.

Accustomed to doing battle in the expanse of the North Pacific, the fish literally obliterated its stream confines. Yet the flyline remained tight, and the backing hummed with the tension of a charged high-voltage cable. For 10, 20, 30 minutes, Sanchez persevered through the toughest antics and maneuvers the king could dish out.

An hour later, the battle had sizzled down to a standoff, with neither side giving nor taking ground. It was that last burst of determination, the desire to win that spurred Sanchez to reach out and tail the salmon, a blush-hued 60-pounder. Could he do it a second time? How about a third or a fourth?

In what seemed to be a Herculean effort for a fly rodder, Sanchez took advantage of Alaska's 21 hours of daylight and virtually fished himself into oblivion. There's no denying he lost plenty of fish. Heavy-duty hooks broke or straighten. Twenty-pound leaders were chewed in half. On one 50-pound fish, his 10-weight rod snapped like a toothpick. But he persevered, and learned the intricacies of catching and battling fly-caught chinooks.

Five days later, Sanchez packed what was left of his rods and tackle and headed home. But one couldn't help but notice his ever so slight, ear-to-ear grin. During his stay he had successfully hooked and landed 76 kings, nearly all ranging from 30 to 60 pounds.

Months later, Sanchez received official notification from the National Freshwater Fishing Hall of Fame: he had swept all the line-class fly fishing categories from 2 to 16-pound tippet, as well as the unlimited tippet category.

Indeed, fly fishing for Alaska kings is the sport of preference for anglers who crave a power-packed angling adventure. Give a king your hardest hookset, and the reaction will be multiplied by a factor of 10. Expect smashed knuckles, cramped arms and backs, and hour-long battles that crumple the strongest wills into humbled

Fly fisherman Dale Anderson reaches for a Susitna River tributary king salmon that took a chartreuse marabou muddler. Use care when landing fly-caught kings, as most are lost at the angler's feet.

submission. Indeed, fly fishing for Alaska king salmon is no romp in the park; each encounter is a full-fledged battle. Success demands that anglers possess the necessary strategy, skill and endurance, reinforced with a massive dose of luck.

Guide Jim Bailey has spent a decade eliminating the "luck" aspect of fly fishing for kings. It was no accident that his lodge is in the heart of some of the best fly fishing for king salmon in the entire state. Rick Sanchez proved that with his record sweep.

"The run of salmon we receive in one particular upper Susitna tributary is the third largest in the entire Susitna drainage," Bailey said. "Starting around June 26 and lasting through mid July, several thousand kings move up these and other nearby creeks. The king fishing during that time is unbelievable. During the peak of the run, anglers can catch from 10 to 20 kings per day."

During early to mid July, streams of the Talkeetna and Susitna drainages are often packed with migrating king salmon. Best catches occur during early morning and late evening hours.

Bailey speaks from experience, and Alaska Department of Fish and Game figures back up his claim. The Susitna Drainage, which includes the Talkeetna River tributary, is one of the largest recreational fisheries in Alaska. But it wasn't always so. The northern Cook Inlet commercial fishery was closed from 1963 to 1985 to rebuild stocks depleted due to overfishing. Sportfishing began in 1979, with a limited commercial fishery allowed in 1986. In recent years, anglers have experienced some of the best fishing on record. Total effort has exceeded 287,000 angler hours, with over 17,600 fish kept by anglers and nearly 33,000 caught and released, per year. Much of this effort takes place in the lower drainages, and consists primarily of bait and spin fishermen. It is in the upper tributaries that fly fishermen and ultralight purists find few if any crowds, and more fish than they can ever hope to catch.

But seeing is believing. In a Piper Super Cub, Bailey flew us over one of many Susitna and Talkeetna tributaries. On one stream, the sight was enough to cause palpitations of the fish-induced kind. Several hundred kings were concentrated in pools and holding in various runs. Five brown bears, ranging from cubs to a respectable eight-footer, were fishing or lounging on the sandbars.

"The bears aren't much of a problem," Bailey said. "They have their established fishing holes, and we have ours. So that our fly fishermen can fish with peace of mind, I'm always nearby with a 375 H&H Magnum rifle, just in case one of the bears is having a bad day. In the 12 years I've been here, we haven't had a confrontation yet, and I intend to keep it that way."

Clint Elston smiles as he attempts to repair several fly and casting rods that were broken during a week of unbelievable king salmon fishing. Big river chinooks are tough on tackle, and the wise angler always takes back-up rods.

Bailey also has a sense of humor. When a woman asked about floating down one of the streams for kings, he asked if she ever played volleyball.

"Sure," she replied.

"No, I don't mean the game volleyball, I mean being THE volleyball," he said. "You go floating around a bend on that stream during this time of year, and I guarantee you'll bump right into a big brown bear standing in mid river. He'll think you're invading his fishing hole and will become mighty upset. With one swipe of his paw you, and the raft, will be that volleyball."

"Seriously, because of the bears we keep our rafting down to a minimum during king season. There's no need for it. Most of our fly fishing for kings is done within a one-mile stretch of the stream. Wading is easy, and water is no more than a couple of feet deep. And it's seldom an angler has to leave a hole, unless a fish is dragging him downstream. There's always a steady supply of kings moving through."

Sanchez agrees, saying most of his fish were caught from a couple of favorite holes.

"Sight casting to these huge kings gives you a big advantage," Sanchez said. "Polarized glasses enable you to pinpoint the largest fish in the pool, and entice them into striking. I found fishing the fly in short twitches, or on a dead drift in chutes with strong current, worked best for me. As far as I'm concerned, fly fishing these clearwater mountain streams is the only way to fish for king salmon. Add the rugged mountain scenery and the bears, wolves,

eagles, moose and caribou, and it's a super outdoor experience."

Veteran fly fisherman and *Sports Afield* fishing editor Tony Acer-rano of Missoula, Montana spent five days fly fishing the clearwater Susitna drainages for king salmon. He, too, became a convert.

"The power these fish have is incredible, and will make mincemeat out of all but the most stout fly tackle," Acerrano said. He advises anglers to take ample flies, leader material and several back-up rods and reels, and lots of film and quality raingear.

He cautioned, however, that even when kings are plentiful, water conditions and time of day dictate whether or not anglers will catch large numbers of fish.

"The best holding areas are calm, deep pools with short, inter-connecting runs," Acerrano said. "In high-water years, often you have no choice but to fish the fast water. Then, you best have plenty of backing and a hefty 10 or 12-weight rod to turn the fish."

Acerrano speaks from experience. I gave him one of my proven king patterns, pointed to the fish most likely to be caught, and waited patiently on a nearby rock. He hooked a king on the first cast, but lost it. He quickly hooked another, and I watched him chase it down stream for a quarter mile as fast as he could run.

When he splashed into the water at what we call "Standoff Point" (aptly named, because it was impossible to follow the fish down any farther, due to deep water) he had less than 10 yards of backing on his reel. He managed to gain line in a muscle-wretching tug-of-war battle which lasted for over 20 minutes. The fish was a respectable 40-pounder.

Acerrano was a sight after he released his king. He had lost his cap, and his sunglasses were dangling from a spare pocket. His

Choosing the right king salmon fly depends on water clarity, time of day, water temperature and position of the fish. The best overall flies incorporate plenty of tinsel and mylar for flash, with a main body of fluorescent chenile, yarn or marabou.

Opposite page: Big king salmon on a fly can make a stiff-spined 10-weight bend with respect. During peak migration times on several Susitna tributaries, top fishermen catch from 10 to 20 kings per day.

blond hair was tousled into a birdnest and his leader looked as if it was passed through a grater. After a photo sequence, a trademark surfaced that is common among successful king salmon fly fishers: that ear-to-ear grin.

"I've fished for salmon and trout all over Canada and the Lower 48, and sight casting flies for trophy king salmon is fabulous sport. My favorite part was watching that 40-pounder surge after and grab the fly. It adds new dimension to the sport, and is something every fly fisherman should experience at least once in his or her lifetime."

Yet Acerrano offers advice to those who would follow him. "Fishing the out-of-the-way tributaries of the Susitna is a trip for only the experienced angler who is up-to-date on wilderness survival skills.

"You'll have no contact with civilization until the charter operator returns to pick you up. It's much simpler to use a guide. That way, all the logistics such as transportation, meal preparation and camp chores are taken care of, which means more time for fishing. And believe me, when the river is full of big kings, that's all you want to do."

So remember. If at some time in the near future you tire of catching pip-squeak trout and panfish on miniscule flies you can barely see, consider a fly fishing excursion to Alaska's remote Susitna River tributaries for arm-jarring, rooster-tailing, acrobatic king salmon. But first, spend a few months at the nearest gym for a workout of arm curls and laps around the track. When they run 30 to 60 pounds, Alaska's King of the Flies require every bit of swat power you can muster.

Planning Your Trip

WHEN TO GO
Kings start arriving in the middle Susitna and Upper Talkeetna drainages in mid June, and usually peak during the first half of July. For pinkish-chrome fish, plan your trip around June 20th. Later-run fish are more numerous, but darker in color. Expect good fishing for sockeye salmon and grayling, and good fishing for rainbow trout up to 25 inches.

WHAT TO TAKE
Use at least a 10-weight, 9 1/2-foot graphite or IMX rod with a fighting butt. The reel with the most muscle for handling these bruiser kings is an Alvey 425 saltwater fly reel. It has a perfect drag system suited for big kings, and it has landed several hundred salmon for me without a single malfunction. Take several extra spools. Start out with a sink-tip line, or floating line with mini lead heads. In many areas, a floating line and weighted fly is all that's required. You'll need at least 200 yards of 30-pound backing. Expect to lose tackle.

Neoprene waders are a must, as are polarized sunglasses. A braided leader system offers quick change-overs to meet water conditions. For the most part, however, you'll be fishing a 24-to 36-inch leader of 17-to 20-pound Maxima or Dai Riki.

My favorite king flies include Klutina King Killer, Fat Freddie, Baker Buster, Maraflash, Alaskabou and Animated Alevin. Alaska Perry Flies in fluorescent red, chartreuse and orange are effective on dark days, when plenty of flash is required.

HOW TO GET THERE
From Anchorage International Airport, most lodge owners on the upper Susitna and Talkeetna rivers will provide transportation to and from their lodge. Once there, they'll provide daily transportation via air or boat to the fishing hotspots. Do-it-yourselfers should plan on riverboat or fly-in access via charter operations based out of Talkeetna, Willow or Anchorage. Oftentimes you can save money by taking a bus or van to Talkeetna, and chartering from there. Check with the bus lines for specific schedules.

WHERE TO STAY
Several lodges offer complete accommodations, including meals and guide service, in remote as well as congested areas. One guide has exclusive rights to access land not available to the general public. Charter operators offer a few tent camps, however, for truly remote fishing, be prepared to camp out on your own. Bears are often a problem on many salmon streams, and campers should be well versed in bear avoidance and protection. A .338 or larger caliber rifle, as well as whistles and

Chris Batin with a 45-pound king salmon that took a weighted orange and silver fly. The salmon took over an hour to land, and the 20-pound tippet was badly frayed from the numerous runs the fish made through nearby riffles. The fish was released.

bells, are what I personally use when fishing bear-infested salmon streams.

APPROXIMATE COST

A five-day, four-night stay at a lodge in this area can run approximately $1700 per person; a three-day adventure costs $1000. This includes round-trip transportation to the lodge, all meals, guides and accommodations. River-based (boat access only) lodges are slightly less. For fly-out charters, rates vary according to aircraft used. Figure at least $250 per hour.

WHO TO CONTACT

For a listing of guides, outfitters and do-it-yourself services, turn to page 208, "Free Information To Plan Your Trip."

3 Adventure

Fishing under the brooding countenance of Mount Peulik, located in the Becharof National Wildlife Refuge.

Naknek's October Rainbows

FISHING FOR OCTOBER RAINBOWS on the Naknek River in Southwest Alaska is not a sport for the weak of heart. Icy droplets of rain driven by gale-force winds, clouds of biting black gnats, and hours upon hours of casting all take their toll on the angler. But the rewards are usually worth the discomforts.

For here you'll find rainbows with a warrior's physique acquired after dining on helping after helping of salmon egg omelet served on the gravel substrates of the Naknek. These are no ordinary rainbows of the type found in the Lower 48, but rather, fish with belligerence and stamina. They spread out in a river like soldiers on a battlefield, each taking a position behind a rock or barrier that offers the best angle of attack.

Victory for Naknek's October rainbows is not in conquering the thousands of sockeye salmon that are digging redds ahead of them, but rather, in acquiring the fruits of their labors, the spoils of war in this annual battle of survival. The salmon need to lay their eggs to perpetuate the species; the rainbows, to capture and eat the eggs in order to survive the winter.

Come with me, friend, to observe this spectacle first-hand. It won't be easy. The alder and willow thickets make for tough going.

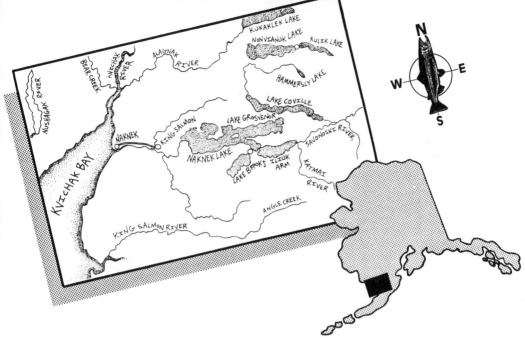

Brush ensnares fly line and leader, and beaver-chewed aspens gouge at vulnerable neoprene waders. Those birds you see skittering about are willow ptarmigan, changing from summer brown to winter white. Another 200 yards and we'll be there.

The spawning bed is a wide stretch of shallow riffles and gravel bars dotted with the reddish forms of sockeyes. On several occasions, I have observed one-on-one combat, where a salmon charges a rainbow that ventures too near. Rainbow aficionados don't find the sight too pleasant. The salmon grabs the rainbow and buries its curved teeth into the trout's flesh. The rainbow struggles wildly to escape, and as a result, drives the salmon's teeth deeper into its skin. The trout breaks free, scratched and perhaps missing a few scales. We can hope the fish is a bit more battle-wary.

See how the trout wait patiently for the salmon to release their eggs? Most of the eggs go into the redds the females have dug. However, many break free, tumbling downstream. Then the feeding frenzy begins, as rainbow, grayling and char battle for the spoils. It's wonder enough to watch this event take place. It's Nature's foremost privilege to actually take part in it; to duel it out with a rainbow on the end of a 6-weight fly rod and egg pattern.

The feat is not as easy as it sounds. Like veteran warriors, October rainbows are strategists in stream warfare. Once hooked, they employ whatever tactics are necessary to sever your control of them. The larger ones refuse to consider carelessly presented flies and lures. Even properly presented flies are often ignored by battle-wise veterans. Such is the nature of the fish. But for the angler alert to these various strategies, the battle for October rainbows can be won.

A Glo-Bug is very effective in catching rainbows during salmon spawning time. The pattern imitates a salmon egg, a food item that quickly puts pounds on wild rainbows and helps them survive the long Alaska winter.

Opposite page: An aerial view of Naknek sockeye salmon milling around their spawning area. Concentrations of salmon serve as a biological magnet, attracting rainbow and char to feed on the eggs and carcasses.

Larry Suiter makes a living as a fishing guide on the Naknek River. He won't say fishing for October rainbows is easy. He knows the fish are finicky, and that the truly large trout do not come every other cast.

"Catching October rainbows requires lots of hard work," he says. "But the fish are there. It's just a matter of finding them, and enticing them to strike. Last October, one of my clients caught and released 24 rainbows in a single day. The largest went 15 pounds."

Normally, heavy fishing pressure can cause Naknek rainbows to develop a severe case of lockjaw. According to Alaska Department of Fish and Game biologists, the area around King Salmon is receiving more and more fishing pressure during summer as anglers discover the variety of fishing the Naknek offers.

But in October, the pressure is minimal when compared to other fisheries in the state. For instance, during one recent fishing trip the first week in October, I observed less than 12 people fishing a five-mile stretch of the Naknek. That's enough elbow room for me, especially if the quarry is slab-sided 'bows.

Anglers can enjoy even less fishing pressure if they're willing to fly out to the Alagnak or smaller tributaries. As Suiter and I flew the Cessna 185 to a remote tributary north of Becharof, he filled me in on the Naknek fishery below us.

"The truly large rainbows spend the summer months in Naknek River and lake," he said. "Fishing starts improving as the sockeyes start spawning, and the availability of free-floating eggs increase.

Barry Leeds with his trophy rainbow of a lifetime, a 32-inch, 14-pounder caught north of the Naknek River.

The fishing peaks when the salmon start dying off, and the big 'bows look for schools of sockeye or silver salmon. They're also migrating to their overwintering areas, which means big rainbows become available to anglers."

"How big is big?"

Suiter shrugged. "We'll soon find out."

That afternoon, under beams of warm sunshine, fishing action was consistent, with Suiter and I hooking and releasing rainbows from four to eight pounds. We didn't catch any 18 pounders his clients have hooked in the past, but we did land one that exceeded 10. Best of all, there wasn't another soul around.

As we took time for lunch at stream's edge, we continued to discuss this fishery.

"Few anglers inside and outside Alaska take advantage of this excellent watershed this time of year," Suiter said. "As we experienced this morning, one of the joys of fishing for October rainbows is drifting a salmon egg pattern down a side riffle, on either side of a school of spawning sockeye salmon. They really smack it, or suck it in so lightly you won't even know a fish is on."

"I had a few of those on myself today," I said as I examined my tattered collection of egg patterns.

"However, anglers shouldn't expect fishing to be excellent all the time," Suiter added. "A lack of salmon, a cold front moving through, or just plain finickiness of the fish, will also cause them to ignore the most carefully presented fly or lure. Then, it's time to start scouting for receptive fish."

The next day a storm had moved in, and the 'bows were holding deep. Rather than fly-out, we boated to the middle Naknek. Suiter unpacked a box of plugs he uses to backtroll for lunker rainbows.

When rainbow trout are mixed with schools of salmon, fish the tail end and open areas of the school. Because salmon are very aggressive and grow sharp teeth for defense, smaller rainbows avoid injury by darting into a school only when eggs are available.

His favorites are Storm Wee Warts in gold, fluorescent pink, and green. Suiter prefers the rattle models over the non-rattle types, arguing that the rainbows can home-in on the sound. And he'll rig each one to run on single hooks, rather than the factory-equipped trebles, to facilitate ease of releasing fish.

"We don't want anglers to rape the fishery," Suiter said. "Anglers should expect to catch-and-release most of their fish. If they catch a true hog, it can be kept for the wall. Even then, we push for fiberglass replicas."

Because a portion of the Naknek River is influenced by tidal fluctuations, Suiter employs conventional trolling techniques when the current is slow or non-existent due to an incoming or high tide. During low tide, or in areas with a greater current flow, backtrolling works best.

I remembered a conversation I had with guide Dan Meyers earlier that day. He believes fishing technique is only half the battle. Finding the fish is often the most difficult part of fishing for Naknek rainbows. Meyers prefers to fish in select holes that he has personally found to be productive. Whether you are fishing flies or plugs, here's what he recommends: Look for runs along sandbars, channels near shore, and flat areas near grassy sloughs. He avoids the deep, main channel of the Naknek, as the current is usually too fast to hold large rainbows.

Suiter was asked, where would a newcomer look first if he were to fish the Naknek?

"Try the side currents, where the 'bows can easily dart out and grab a salmon egg or unsuspecting sculpin," he said. "Mostly, however, you'll find them close to sockeye salmon. Find the sockeye schools, and you'll find rainbows nearby."

An October rainbow takes to the air. As a general rule, rainbows gorged on eggs seldom jump, preferring to bulldog for bottom when hooked. Leaner bows seem to be more acrobatic.

Opposite page: Rainbows are not the only sportfish species feeding on salmon eggs. Here, Larry Suiter shows a fine grayling he caught in early August.

The wind had finally died down, allowing us to fly fish for the big 'bows. As the sun burned off the gray clouds, I observed numerous sockeyes in the clear currents of the Naknek. Suiter is also an advocate of catching rainbows on flies, especially Glo-Bugs, a proper name for salmon-egg imitating fuzz balls. He says the most effective colors are peach and fluorescent red.

"The rainbows tore up my entire supply of Glo-Bugs last week," he said. "I had to fly my plane into town and purchase more. And that's all the way to Anchorage, a five-hour flight. Fall rainbows are hard on flies."

Suiter said experimentation is the key when it comes to catching October rainbows. As the month wears on, and the sockeye salmon become spawned out, the rainbows will turn to other food items such as mice.

"One morning, a friend of mine caught a rainbow on a drowned mouse pattern," he said. "The rainbow had four mice in its stomach. He prefers to dead drift the pattern along the edge of grass and sandy flats, where mice and voles are usually found. The Minky Mouse pattern catches fish, and large ones at that."

Other patterns that work well include an egg-sucking leech, green-butted skunk, polar shrimp, and sculpin patterns. A sink-tip or heavy, 400-grain nymphing line is a must for fishing the fast currents of the Naknek. In the shallower side currents, a floating line with a weighted fly works well. Also expect to catch grayling and char on the same patterns.

The next morning was not the best for rainbow fishing. Thirty mile-per-hour winds, with gusts to 50 m.p.h., blew from the south and white-capped the river. Any type of fishing was impossible, with the exception of those told in stories at the bar in the Quinnat Landing Hotel.

"Bad weather is usually what keeps most anglers at home in

Anchorage," Suiter said. "If they knew what they were missing, they'd be down here, waiting for the weather to lift. Once it does, the fishing is usually very good."

The following morning, the wind was still blowing, but had died down enough to load the gear into the boat and head up the Naknek. In sections of the river protected from the wind, the black gnats were such a nuisance as to make concentration on presenting a fly all but impossible. Suiter turned a few fish, but overall, action was slow. The fish were holding deep, and Suiter wasn't one to waste time changing tactics.

We started fishing near the public boat launch. Within two hours, we had caught and released 14 rainbows, the largest being four pounds. The lunkers were avoiding us. And the wind had picked up force again, causing the river to whitecap.

I was pleased with the action, but Suiter said the weather was responsible for the lull in fish activity.

"Tomorrow, we'll hit a series of riffles I know a few miles downriver," he said. "If the weather cooperates, we'll hook a hog."

The next day, the wind had died to a whisper, and the gnats were again out in force.

Autumn was manifest in its glory that day on the Peninsula. Three other boats were on the five-mile stretch of river we were fishing; not crowded, by any means. Gold and rust-colored leaves glistened in the morning dew. Ptarmigan clucked their reorganization calls in the shoreline alders, while fly lines zipped through the guides with seemingly little effort. The only thing missing were the rainbows, and they were on order.

The riffles had been a good choice. Suiter landed several rainbows in the 30-inch class on a leech pattern. Using an ultralight outfit, my brother Joe wrestled in a 18-inch grayling, followed by a chunky, eight-pound rainbow, the fattest fish of the day. He released it, rather slowly, but with a smile. He would settle for a fiberglass replica.

After catching additional rainbows ranging from two to six pounds, we called it a morning and headed in for lunch. Fishing had been good, and reports from other anglers on the river indicated that they, too, had done well in the early-morning hours. But like too many fishing trips, the action starts to pick up when it's time to leave, and we were scheduled to head back to Fairbanks that afternoon.

October rainbow fishing on the Naknek offers no guarantee of success in catching that coveted 30-inch, 14-pound rainbow. You can, however, expect trout action that is seldom surpassed in other watersheds, as well as a panorama of splendid fall colors. I can't think of a better time or place to catch that trophy rainbow trout.

Planning Your Trip

WHEN TO GO

Late September through October offers the best fishing for large rainbows. Anglers should plan on spending no less than three days, preferably five to make up for interruptions due to inclement weather commonplace during that time of year.

WHAT TO TAKE

A parka that allows freedom of movement and casting. Neoprene waders, as well as gloves, are imperative. Always carry a small vacuum bottle of hot liquid and a daypack packed with lunch and emergency food should you suffer a boat breakdown. An emergency pack which includes matches, space blanket and fire starter is also wise.

An 8-weight rod is my favorite, as the extra muscle helps in casting large mouse and attractor flies in the strong wind. Egg patterns in peach, salmon roe, apricot and pink are best, as are black marabou muddlers, woolly buggers, egg-sucking leeches, and flesh flies in white and pink.

HOW TO GET THERE

Fly commercial airlines to Anchorage, with a connecting flight to King Salmon. Airlines frequently offer discount rates for travel during late September and October. Check with several companies before purchasing your tickets, and be sure you inquire about return travel should your bush plane flight be delayed due to bad weather.

WHERE TO STAY

Fishing in the Peninsula's inclement weather is trying enough without having to camp in it at day's end. Rent a motel room for several days in King Salmon. Rental boats are available in King Salmon.

APPROXIMATE COSTS

A week-long rainbow fishing package, complete with boat and accommodations, start at $1,000. Fly outs to nearby rivers and creeks are extra, and worth the expense. Although usually smaller in size, trout, as well as grayling and char, are often more plentiful on smaller creeks accessible by fly-out, for those fly fishermen wishing fish-a-cast action. A few that I've experienced offer world-class angling opportunities.

WHO TO CONTACT

For a comprehensive listing of guides, outfitters and do-it-yourself services, turn to page 208, "Free Information To Plan Your Trip."

4 Adventure

Anglers enjoying a June day fishing for char on Lake Beverley, one of the state's best char fisheries located in the Wood-Tikchik chain.

Tikchik Char Extravaganza

DAYS ARE LONG IN ALASKA, but this day was too long. Perhaps it was the summer equinox that made it unbearable, or the subsequent 19 hours of daylight that beat mercilessly upon the land. Maybe the 85-degree temperature was to blame. No matter. I would not see the comfort of nightfall. Draped in a heavy orange shroud, the midnight sun hovered above the northern horizon. It seemed to flicker, just for a second, as it touched a snow-capped peak. And like a match that suddenly bursts into flames, the glowing orb came back to life, rising above the mountains, bathing everything in a floodlight of orange. It was the start of another day.

I had dozed off for minutes, perhaps an hour. I don't know how long. Time is meaningless in seemingly perpetual daylight. I awoke to a cool breeze gently rocking the boat. With the momentary reprieve of the sun's fury, it was as if Nature had given a sigh of relief with a warm, caressing breath, delicately fragranced with the scent of cottonwood and fireweed. I rubbed my eyes, and gazed toward shore. I shivered with apprehension as I scanned the dense vegetation of the banks. Mosquitoes, millions of them, waited in ambush in the greenery. Sleep was impossible on shore, and the only alternative was my anchorage at the mouth of the Agulukpak

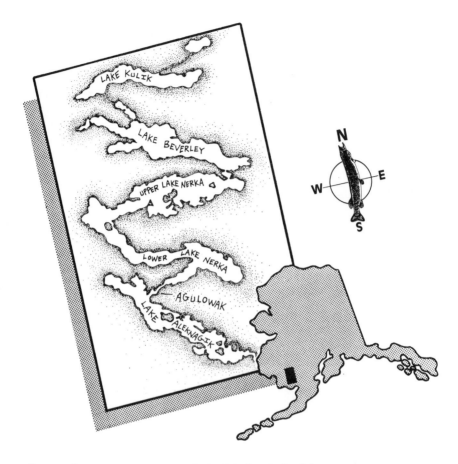

River where it empties into Lake Nerka. It had been a good choice.

The very sight of the river made me forget about the mosquitoes. It was classic trout water. About a mile upstream, the Agulukpak's mouth—nearly a quarter-mile wide—thirstily gulped thousands of gallons of water a minute from Lake Beverley. Farther on down, rock cataracts cleaved the river into a hodge-podge of irregular segments. Each section was ablaze with the vibrant orange of the midnight sun, which irradiated the greens and blues of the gravel substrate and tinged the mist that slowly settled in. But I was not after rainbow trout, even though they were present. I was waiting for something far better.

Then a shrill cry high above the trees was soon joined by another and another. Suddenly the sky was alive with darting terns and gulls, their plumage bathed in a golden light. They plunged mercilessly into the river, bobbed up, and took to wing for a repeat performance. The flailings of wings and bird bodies resembled a feathery tornado that was about to engulf me in its fury.

45

In June and July, huge schools of char holding at lake outlets push out-migrating smolt to the surface and gorge on the two to four-inch fish. The feeding frenzy of jumping fish attracts gulls (opposite page) to the scene. During peak migration periods, a fish a cast is common.

Within seconds, the avian whirlwind was upon me. The gulls whirled around in circles, while the terns dropped from the sky, screaming with crazed delight. I lowered my head for protection. It was then I saw them. The water surrounding the boat was a living mass of silver. Thousands upon thousands of salmon smolt were frantically zipping out of the river into the protective confines of the lake. I could see the smolts rise up in a current boil and become trapped beneath the surface, where the gulls and terns picked off two and three at a time. Soon the four-inch smolts began jumping frantically out of the water, several into my boat. As I tossed them back in, my eyes widened at the scenario taking place beneath the surface. Thick-bodied char raced through the schools of smolt with endless energy. The water looked as if a can of glitter had been spilled. The fish were even engulfing the scales.

I didn't need more convincing. I had waited all day for what was taking place. I stripped out line and cast my smolt pattern into the pool. It was an instantaneous pick-up. The reel screamed in unison with the gulls. The char zipped under the surface, catching the attention of a few birds. They hovered momentarily over the fish.

"Buzz off," I said. "This is my fish. Pick on a fish you can handle." With that, the birds flew off, probably out of impatience rather than at my admonitions.

The char dove for the sanctuary of the lake bottom, where it slugged it out in a lengthy series of body rolls and head shakes. Minutes later, I wrestled the pot-bellied fish to the surface. It regurgitated a handful of smolt, which were immediately consumed by other fish and gulls. I eased the char to hand. Its golden-yellow flanks were adorned with pink, thumbnail-size circles. There were several external parasites protruding from its cream-colored back. Each fin was a dark brown, with the outer edge highlighted with a heavy band of white. The char chomped on my fly several times, as if chastising it for interrupting its midnight meal.

"Off you go, water tiger," I said, releasing the fish. "I have a couple more char to catch." The char dove for bottom, and smolt scurried across the surface.

"Couple" was an understatement. The smolt migration lasted until 4 a.m. By then I had caught at least 70 char ranging from 4 to 10 pounds, and I was practicing restraint in my fish-catching. When the plane came to pick me up several hours later, I was babbling something about how the char were as bad as the mosquitoes in draining an angler's strength.

Arctic char will do that to you, though. My philosophy is that if

47

you want to be in prestigious company, mingle with rainbow trout. If you want a heavyweight bout, spar a few rounds with a king salmon. Grayling offer aristocratic finesse that the purist types appreciate. But if you want hard-core fishing action, the never-ending type that produces sportfish burn-out in the most fervent of anglers, pursue arctic char.

The arctic char is the most northerly of all salmonids and is circumpolar in distribution. The most abundant populations exist in Alaska, where the species can be found from the Aleutian islands north into Bristol Bay and up around the coast into Canadian waters. Isolated populations can also be found in select interior lakes and the colder, deeper lakes of the Kenai Peninsula.

Many anglers confuse Dolly Varden char with arctic char. There's much to be confused about. The physical characteristics of both fish are so similar that even trained fisheries biologists often have difficulty in identifying variations of either species. As a rule, arctic char have 23 to 32 gill rakers on the left gill arch, while Dolly Varden have anywhere from 17 to 23. The spots on the flank of the fish are another identifying aid. A Dolly's are usually smaller than the pupil of the eye, while on an arctic char they are larger than the pupil.

Biologists are still uncertain as to whether true arctic char are either anadromous or strictly freshwater species. I feel—along with many biologists—that all arctic char within Alaska are technically freshwater lake and river dwellers. While the species has been reported as being anadromous from Bristol Bay to Barter Island, numerous reports and research investigations have indicated these fish to be the northern form of the Dolly Varden. Other biologists will argue that Alaska char are definitely anadromous, as there are anadromous char populations in Canada, Europe and Siberia. Opinions vary as to the extent of this saltwater lifestyle. Some say char stay in freshwater regions of intertidal areas and never fully enter a saline environment, while others believe char travel great distances along shoreline routes. Enough. Until more research is done on char, this subject will definitely remain a gray area in fisheries biology. Keep in mind that when both share the same watershed, the techniques that catch one will catch the other.

Many anglers make the mistake of comparing arctic char fishing with Lower 48 trout fishing. I've seen crack trout anglers—who can hold their own on any of the West's blue ribbon trout streams—fall flat on their faces when it comes to figuring out arctic char. This is easy to explain. Success in arctic char fishing is dependent upon understanding the life cycle and habits of salmon, in both their smolt and spawning phases of life. On the Agulukpak, these phases can best be broken into two time frames: spring and fall.

This arctic char inhaled a Coronation, a generic smolt pattern used during early spring and summer. When char are holding in rivers, stripping the fly across the surface, with frequent pauses so the fly can flutter in the current, draws the hardest strikes.

SPRING

As soon as ice-out hits the lower Wood River-Tikchik lakes, salmon smolt begin their out-migration to the sea. Lake outlets and inlets—especially those emptying watersheds that host salmon spawning activity later in the year—are concentration points for smolts and char. Yet, most anglers never witness a smolt migration. Most take place between the hours of 10 p.m. and 4 a.m. In test studies done by ADF&G, nearly 95 percent of the smolts collected for survey were caught from 9 p.m. to 2 a.m. The second best time is from 9 p.m. to 11 p.m. My own catch statistics show that on dark, cloudy days, out-migrations often start as early as 7 p.m.

Some of my best fishing for char have been long after most anglers have turned in for the day. For nearly a week, friend Tony Acerrano and I fished the Peace River for arctic char in late June. The type of fishing we experienced is commonplace during the smolt migration, providing you know what to use and how to fish.

Under overcast skies there was barely light enough to see, but this didn't affect us or the char fishing. We motored the small boat down the lake and to the outlet, and anchored near an abrupt drop-off. We didn't see any char jumping or chasing smolt, but we knew they were holding near the deep drop-off. The water boiled up from the depths in a nearly inaudible hiss, like a slow leak from a tire.

The technique was simple. With ultralight rods and four-pound test, we cast out, and tightlined the lure as it dropped. That evening, the strikes were easy to detect, as the char hit our offerings with gusto. Even in the eerie glow of twilight, we had fish on nearly every cast.

After catching 10 to 15 fish each, Tony and I would pull over to

49

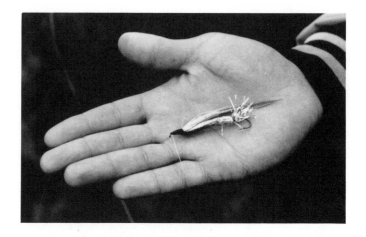

A variation of a blue smolt pattern. Tie the pattern with a few wraps of lead wire underneath the mylar tubing. Fish this with a long leader and floating fly line, twitching the fly as the current carries it through a smolt pond.

shore, take a swig of brandy to warm up and talk about fish won and lost, childhood pranks, lost loves and other topics men discuss while fishing a remote river. Eventually, the action slowed, and we motored back to camp. In several hours, we would awaken to fish for char during the daylight hours.

Daylight fishing action in the Tikchik chain—especially during peak migrations—can fluctuate. It can be as good as the evening fishery, or extremely poor. One reason for the drop in activity is that during daylight, very few smolt out-migrate. Observations made at Lake Aleknagik show that sockeye smolt tend to behave in a manner supporting what is known as the "reservoir hypothesis." Smolt will concentrate in shallow sections of the lake, especially those near the lake's outlet. There, the young salmon hide from char and trout, which are generally cruising in slightly deeper water. Occasionally a char will dart in and grab a smolt, creating feeding rings and splashes that can be seen from afar. However, when avian predation is heavy, smolt will find sanctuary in deep water. This trait is known as a vertical migration. Unless you're equipped with a sonar unit, it's tough to find concentrations of smolt and char that have suspended in the deep-water lakes of this lake system.

For the most fun and success, fish the lower lakes in the chain from mid June through early to mid July. There, smolt are the first to out-migrate, sometimes immediately after ice-out.

If you miss the first run, don't despair. When the ice melts in the upper lakes, the smolts there will begin their run down through the chain. Then, the lake's inlet—especially during early morning—produces the best fishing of the day. On cloudy days, smolts group up, and travel is kept to a minimum.

Once you've found the smolt, chances are you've found the char.

Lodge owner Ken Stockholm, left, and Chris Batin compare arctic char they caught while fishing the Wood River-Tikchik State Park in late July. One fish was caught on a small Kastmaster, while the other was caught on a two-egg marabou. Spawning sockeye were nearby.

Unless you can see surface activity, start deep and fish to shallow. The bigger char tend to hold deep, while the smaller fish cruise beneath the surface.

Whenever a smolt stream empties into a lake, you'll invariably find what I call a "smolt pond." These are common in the Wood-Tikchik chain. A smolt pond is a glassy area of water, usually situated in the current, and consists of water dropping off a ledge and impacting a house-size boulder or similar structure. Smolt get trapped in the rising currents, where char are always waiting for an easy meal.

Here's how to fish a smolt pond: Cast to the outside edge of this pool, and quickly twitch the lure back to the boat. About half way up, quickly lower your rod tip, dropping the lure a couple of feet. The current will usually carry the fluttering lure into a feeding lane and an inevitable strike.

Some char will take positions in rivers and streams to wait for out-migrating smolt. This is especially true in outlets lacking structure or currents to concentrate smolt, such as the Peace River. Char take position behind boulders and along the side currents, which are migratory pathways for smolt. Again, fishing is best in the later evening and early morning. However, I've seen the water boil with activity throughout the day at the peak of a migration.

Char usually hold in groups, so where you find one, you may find 50 or hundreds. Approach them from downstream, and cast the fly well past the holding area. Char have good eyesight, and will move into position to intercept the fly if they can see it coming. Action is the key word here, which is why I prefer flies tied with Flashabou or a similar material that pulsate in the slightest current. Twitch the fly across current as it moves into the holding area. I don't recommend dead drifts, especially in low-water conditions, because char have a chance to look the fly over and recognize it as a fake. Keep it moving, and you'll trigger their predatory instinct to strike.

FALL

During late summer and fall, char will do one of two things. Some will remain in the deep-water haunts of a lake and feed on sticklebacks, sculpins and whitefish. Others will follow schools of migrating sockeye salmon through a watershed to their spawning beds, which are usually the littoral areas of the lake system. There, char will take up residence on the outer edge of the salmon schools, waiting to gorge on any free-floating eggs that drift out of the redd. Therefore, find nesting salmon, and you find char.

For instance, on Lake Aleknagik, sockeye salmon play the largest role in feeding schools of arctic char. Millions of salmon enter the Wood River-Tikchik chain through Aleknagik. They mass up in schools along the shoreline. In a few areas, arctic char and Dolly Varden are as numerous, if not more so, than the salmon. The conditions provide for a fly fisherman's delight.

You have two options, depending on the type of water fished. On rivers and streams, fish undercut banks, behind sweepers and in deep holes. There, deep-water char will take an egg or smolt pattern. This is a prime example of the energy expenditure-mass relationship theory. A fish knows instinctively not to expend more energy than it will receive from pursuing and ingesting a food item. Often, the larger the fly, and the closer you present it to the fish, the better your chances of catching it.

I prefer a sink-tip line, with a lead wrap-around near the end for a quicker sink. I rarely go longer than a seven and a half-foot leader, tapered down to 1X. I like the gaudy baitfish patterns such as a Herring or Blue Smolt, and the Coronation when water levels are low.

Allow the fly to sink before twitching it through the pool. Keep it just over bottom. Once the drift is completed, strip the fly upstream in an erratic manner. This best imitates a wounded smolt caught in the current, and is one of the few techniques that will pull up a big char. Strikes are short, so be ready with a hookset at the slightest hesitation.

Later in the season, there'll be times when char want only salmon eggs. They abandon their deepwater hangouts and position themselves in water from four to 12 inches deep. The eggs that wash out of the redd usually drift into shallower water, where char anxiously await to feed on the salmon egg smorgasbord.

It's important to imitate a salmon egg as closely as possible. I favor a Glo-Bug or Two-Egg Marabou. If char are finicky, I add a drop of salmon egg oil to the fly. It often spells the difference between success and failure.

Fishing an egg pattern in shallow water requires a floating line and a dead-drift technique. If the fly is too buoyant, add a strand

Preceeding page: Dolly Varden char also feed heavily on free-drifting salmon eggs. Migrating into freshwater with the salmon, the char remain close by until egg supplies dwindle. In September and October, most char break away and initiate spawning and overwintering migrations.

This page: On the Alaska Peninsula, several watersheds offer fishing for both Dolly Varden and arctic char against a spectacular panoramic backdrop of the Aleutian Range.

or two of lead wire to the shank. Position yourself above a gravel bar or slightly sloping gravel bank and quarter your cast upstream. As the fly drifts past, strip out more line and drift the fly into the shallows directly below you. In slightly turbid water, allow the egg to hang in the current for a few seconds before stripping it back a few feet. Char love this "suspended egg" tactic. Repeat the procedure.

The arctic char is a universal symbol of wildness, of unpolluted waters and the marvel of the midnight sun. Don't ever pass up an opportunity to appreciate first-hand the char's complex lifestyle and fishing action as it exists in the upper Wood-Tikchik lakes system. But for those that do, a word of warning. Fishing afterwards for bass and trout will never be the same. So don't say I didn't warn you!

Planning Your Trip

WHEN TO GO

The best char fishing takes place immediately after ice-out in mid June, and lasts through July. After the smolt run, fishing slacks off as the char redistribute themselves throughout the drainages, congregating near spawning sockeye salmon until late September. The Agulukpak and Agulowak rivers provide excellent fishing in June and through the first week in July. A char per cast is common.

WHAT TO TAKE

For deepwater char, use an ultralight spinning outfit and four to six-pound test, non-fluorescent monofilament line. Fluorescent and fluorescent-clear lines spook char in their extremely clear habitat. Any lure that imitates a smolt—i.e. elongated, with a silvery flash—will catch char. Metal and leadheads are good, as are Fjord spoons and Renosky Laser Spoons.

For flyfishers, take a 6-weight rod with spools of floating and sink-tip line. Pack twice the number of flies you would normally take. I always carry at least five dozen flies and for mid lake fishing, a small tackle box stuffed with 1/32 to 1/2-ounce lures. All lures must carry single, barbless hooks.

Polarized sunglasses, sun tan lotion, mosquito net, insect repellent, ankle-fit hip boots or waders, and a daypack to carry extra jacket. Weather in the area is often inclement, so quality raingear is a must. A boat is preferable, but not essential for fishing success.

HOW TO GET THERE

Take a commercial airline out of Anchorage to Dillingham, and charter with a private carrier to the Wood River-Tikchik system. Depending on gear and length of fly-out, total cost would be between $800 to $1,000 for a group of two to three anglers.

WHERE TO STAY

Camping is permitted in the Wood River-Tikchik State Park and nearby Togiak National Wildlife Refuge. Numerous lodges in the area fish the Tikchik chain, and offer guided, daily fly-out service, meals and accommodations for about $4,000 for a week-long trip.

WHO TO CONTACT

For a listing of guides, outfitters and do-it-yourself services, turn to page 208, "Free Information To Plan Your Trip."

5 Adventure

Fishing in solitude on American Wellesley Lake, located a few miles from the Alaska-Canada border. Access is by float-plane fly-in only.

American Wellesley Pike

I STOOD THERE, waist deep in the horsetail reeds and lily pads of American Wellesley, a fly-in lake located east of Northway, about 12 miles from the Alaska-Canada Border. Even though I was immobile in the water and shin-deep mud, the world continued around me. Water beetles scurried about, their miniature legs stroking the surface like oars. Freshwater scuds darted through weedy caverns, while whitefish dimpled the surface farther out on the lake.

I nodded in appreciation of these sights before concentrating on a single, two-foot area without reeds about 20 feet away. I made a few false casts and dropped the fly into the opening. The red-and-yellow bucktail bug floated high in the water, an easy target in the dim light of pre-dawn. I knew a northern pike was holding near that opening, and my body responded accordingly. Anxiety sensitized my nerve endings. My stomach and internal organs became as weightless as if I were riding down a 10-story roller coaster. And expectation of excitement intensified my lightheadedness.

Three. Two. One. My mental countdown had ended, and it was time to twitch the fly. My mind gave the command, but I was

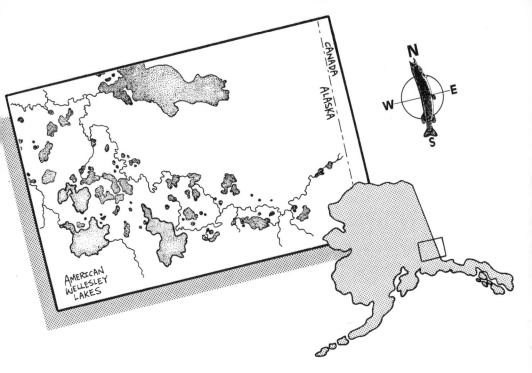

hesitant, knowing what would occur. A surge of will power prevailed, and like a rusty hinge finally breaking free, my forearm twitched to move the fly.

The fly chugged across the opening, rippling the glassy surface. Two feet behind the fly, a swirl formed. Age-yellowed fins broke the surface. Where the fly once was floating, a massive boil erupted, and in its epicenter was the toothy maw of a northern pike.

I set the hook prematurely, jerking the fly out of the fish's mouth. The fly skipped across the surface, and settled upside down. The pike charged it again, leaping horizontally out of the water before coming down on the fly. My entire body tensed to the point of explosion. Anxiety was paramount. I forced myself to count this time. One thousand one. One thousand two.

My arm set the hook with the snap of a coiled spring being released. I felt a good weight at the end of the flyrod. The pike atomized the surface in three massive headshakes before burrowing into the safety of its weed-choked sanctuary.

This was no trophy pike by any means. It was a respectable 12-pounder that thrashed and splashed its displeasure through a series of twists and contortions. I soon had it within range of my needlenose pliers. A quick twist, and the pike swam off into the weeds as if nothing happened. And it was only a matter of a few minutes before my friend, Alan, hooked into a pike of similar size. Before long, we both were into fish, laughing and carrying on as anglers do when they're pike fishing on Alaska's American Wellesley Lake.

Wellesley pike are noted for a diet heavy in forage fish and rodents. A mouse pattern worked slowly along the grassy edges of shoreline can produce explosive strikes.

It's not surprising that many anglers are unfamiliar with American Wellesley. Anglers entering Alaska for the first time via the Alcan Highway miss it on their mad dash for the coast and its glamour species—salmon, halibut, rainbow trout and Dolly Varden.

American Wellesley pike, as do other pike throughout Alaska, have plenty to offer. The pike is an extremely efficient predator that has remained relatively unchanged for more than 60 million years. Its stomach is as indiscriminate as it is insatiable. Some of the standard food items pike regularly feed upon are ducks, muskrats, mice, and birds. In fact, documented cases in Europe have shown pike having attacked foxes and pigs that have ventured too close to the water's edge for that late-night drink!

American Wellesley pike aim to please. They're available all summer long, enticing anglers to try their luck. And luck you'll need, not in catching fish, but in keeping up with the action, providing you know the secret to catching these fish. Let me share some of the tips I've learned over the years.

American Wellesley offers near-perfect pike habitat. Lily pads choke the bays and inlets, and a dense ribbon of weed growth runs the length of the lake's center. Whitefish are abundant, offering a prime forage food base for pike. Best of all, available to anglers is a 16 by 20-foot U.S. Fish and Wildlife Service cabin, complete with stove, bunks, tables, lanterns and cooking utensils. The cabin, which can be rented on a daily or weekly basis, is located on a small bluff overlooking the lake. Two skiffs at the cabin provide access to the many bays, although good fishing can be had by wading the shoreline. The outhouse is in good condition, and the cabin is virtually mosquito-proof.

Many anglers fail to hook pike because they react to the wake and boil, and set the hook too soon. After you see the explosion of water signalling the pike has grabbed the fly, count one-thousand and one before setting the hook. Your hook-ups will increase substantially.

ABOUT THE AREA

Thick stands of spruce cover the rolling hills surrounding the lake. Several feeder streams empty into the lake, creating a good supply of oxygenated water. A proven producer is a small stream located to the right at the cabin, at the head of a bay. It courses through reeds before sweeping over a steep drop-off. Pike are usually holding three to four feet into the rushes, with larger fish waiting at the edge of the drop-off. Despite the conditions, 8 to 10-pound fish frequent here, with smaller fish found back in the weeds.

Continue around the lake to the opposite side of the bay. There, drift with the wind or slow troll while casting along the edge of weedy structure in about 10 feet of water (you can easily see this breakline from the boat as you're drifting). It is common to hook and release from 15 to 20 pike in this stretch.

Lure anglers will find success farther out in the lake in deepwater channels bordering lily pads. Troll one-ounce spoons and diving plugs slowly along weedlines, or cast a Johnson Silver Minnow and pork rind into openings in cover.

Opposite page: Outdoor writer Alan Liere with a northern pike caught within sight of the U.S. Fish and Wildlife Service cabin located on American Wellesley.

Another good location is the weedbeds located around the point from the cabin. Big fish hold tight on the edges of the thick stuff, with plenty of smaller fish pushed into the shoreline vegetation. For reasons I'm not able to determine, the large pike along this stretch seldom strike surface lures or floating bugs, although they do take these offerings elsewhere on the lake.

The best overall lure is a Johnson Silver Minnow with a yellow, six-inch-long pork-rind trailer. This lure is our top producer, and is especially effective in the above-mentioned section of the lake. We use short, six-inch, 15-pound-test black wire leaders. A deer-hair mouse and Dahlberg Diver in orange and yellow are the most effective flies.

On our last trip, we found pike numbers to be poor or non-existent in the northern end of the lake, even though adequate cover was available. We attribute few fish to the relatively shallow water, warm water temperatures and bright sunny days, which kept fish hiding in the acres of lily pads located at the lake's center. On cloudy days, we found fish closer to shore.

Each day, our best fishing occurred from 5 p.m. to 10 p.m. Action was fair for smaller pike at all hours, but the largest pike were caught at twilight in and around shoreline structure. Fishing was also good from 5 a.m. until 9 a.m., after which we had to concentrate our fishing efforts at the center and edges of lily pads.

The lake offered numerous opportunities for exploration, and we saw a variety of wildlife from moose to waterfowl.

Here are a few additional tips for catching American Wellesley pike. Pole a boat as far away from shoreline as possible, but within accurate casting distance. When you see likely looking pike cover—water lilies, sections of reeds, open areas in grass-filled bays—cast

the fly or lure to the base of the shore and slowly retrieve it through cover. If there are no strikes, speed up the lure in increments until it's buzzing the surface. When pike are finicky, they often prefer a fast-moving lure.

Pre-and post-spawning pike are often very territorial. They'll lie dormant in deep-water channels near their spawning grounds, either waiting until their milt or eggs ripen or, after spawning, to regain their strength to resume feeding. Therefore, the best fishing will usually be seven to ten days before the spawn, and immediately after. This can be as late as early June in Alaska, and an excellent time to fish Wellesley.

On any lake with pike, it's important to search out the shallow-water structure, especially those near steep drop-offs and weedbeds. Pike prefer to ambush their prey, and do this by either hiding in available structure or by lying still on the bottom, especially along a migratory pathway used by whitefish or burbot, two species common in Wellesley.

I prefer the deeper water for large pike, especially the depths off rocky points at the opening of weedy bays, and American Wellesley has plenty. There, pike will wait quietly for a fish to pass overhead. The forage fish, or your lure, have little chance of surviving the sudden lunge of a northern at close range. I know ours didn't, and after each trip, we retire a number of lures and flies.

Speed of retrieve is also very important, and should be as slow as possible. Don't be afraid to occasionally lose lures or flies to snags. If you're the type of angler who leaves home with six lures and returns with the same number, you'll never make consistent catches of big pike on Wellesley.

You are fishing the spoon, spinner or plug properly if it's catching weeds and debris from the bottom. Simply clean off the hooks between casts. Remember, the longer a bait stays within the strike zone, the longer it has to trigger a big pike into striking. This holds true especially in shallow water, weedy bays and in water deeper than 10 feet.

After you've hooked that pike, don't allow it to deceive you. It may appear to be sluggish after setting the hook, but watch out! Lunker pike have a habit of using every snag, rock and weedbed to their advantage. So keep that line tight, and watch where the fish is headed every second.

Treat yourself this summer with an affordable, wilderness pike fishing fly-out to American Wellesley Lake. The pike are plentiful and cooperative, the location is remote, and you'll enjoy photographing the wildlife riches of the area, which include moose, bear, swan and beaver. And here's one last tip: take plenty of lures and flies. Wellesley pike chew 'em to shreds. I should know. I speak from experience!

Planning Your Trip

WHEN TO GO

Late June and early July, as well as late August, are prime times to pursue northern pike. However, you can have excellent success throughout the summer, providing you are willing to fish the early morning and late evening time slots, and rest through the mid day lull.

WHAT TO TAKE

Use a rod with plenty of backbone to set the hooks into a lunker pike's maw. I prefer an 8 to 10-weight fly rod with floating line. If spin fishing, take a six-foot, medium-heavy action graphite rod with a level-wind reel capable of holding 200 yards of 12 to 20-pound test monofilament. Use a heavier line when pike are in the weeds.

Keep these tackle tips in mind for pike. Epoxy the screw eyes into your pike plugs. The normal cement used in construction just doesn't hold up. And make sure those hooks are sharp.

If hooks become bent or broken, replace with the same weight or type. Larger or smaller hooks will often throw a plug off balance, making it ineffective.

Effective lures include silver-plated spoons, three-inch gold Dardevles and Norman Weed Walkers.

Flies should be tied with a mono weed guard to minimize hang-ups. Dahlberg divers, chamois leeches, cork popping bugs the size of a quarter and simple streamer flies that are heavy on the flashabou work well.

Wire leaders are a must. I prefer the plastic-coated, black-wire type from 12 to 20-pound test for both fly and spin fishing. Add a net, along with a tube of antibiotic cream for any cuts from the pike's mouthful of sharp teeth, and you're set.

With a 9.9 hp outboard motor, we use about six gallons of gas in three days of fishing. Play it safe and take at least two extra gallons. Also, take along a set of oars to row the boat in and around the weedbeds.

Take along Blazo or Coleman fuel for the cookstove and lanterns, and personal items such as sleeping bags and air mattresses. Silverware and cookware are provided. Take whatever food you desire. Sunscreen is a must-have item.

HOW TO GET THERE

Fly out of Tok or Northway via float-equipped Cessna 185 or 206 aircraft. Book a mid afternoon departure, which allows you enough time to set up camp and prepare dinner before catching the evening bite.

WHERE TO STAY

The USFWS cabin is available via reservation on a first-come, first-served policy. Advance reservations are important, and are usually made by the air charter operator. Do-it-yourself camping is possible, but mosquitoes are ferocious.

APPROXIMATE COSTS

Local air services charge approximately $300 per person, two-person minimum. This includes an outboard for use on the boats, as well as a tank of gasoline.

WHO TO CONTACT

For a listing of guides, outfitters, and do-it-yourself services, turn to page 208, "Free Information To Plan Your Trip."

6 Adventure

A spectacular day float fishing on Beaver Creek, located in the Steese White Mountains a short flight north of Fairbanks.

Beaver Creek Grayling

I HAD JUST RETURNED from a week-long fishing trip pursuing salmon and trout in the Nome area when the phone rang. The caller was my friend, Sharon Durgan Wilson, a writer for the public affairs division of the Bureau of Land Management.

"Are you ready to go grayling fishing?" she asked.

"I've had enough fishing for a while," I replied, tiredly.

"The forecast is for blue skies, and the fish are biting," she said. "A group of us flew out to Beaver Creek last week and we had some excellent grayling fishing. Plus I had a great time floating the river."

It was hard for me to believe that Beaver Creek, a river so close to Fairbanks, could offer excellent grayling fishing. Fair, perhaps. Maybe even good. But excellent? Curiosity got the better of my fatigue.

"Excellent grayling fishing, huh? When do we go?" I queried.

"Tomorrow," she said. "You'll be floating with BLM biologist Winston Hobgood down Beaver Creek. He'll be rowing the inflatable, so you can concentrate on fishing."

We met Winston at an air charter service at Fairbanks International. Adela and I loaded our fishing gear aboard a Helio Courier,

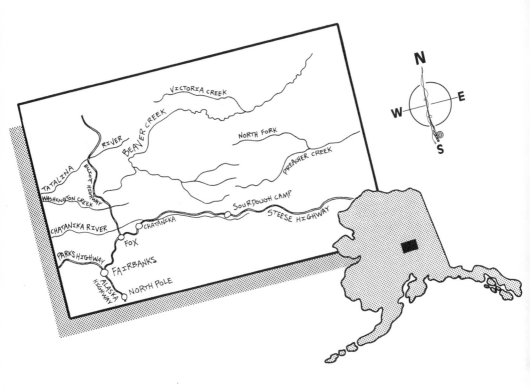

the aircraft of choice for wilderness flying due to its high-performance engine and slow stall speeds.

Rather than fly directly to the creek, however, we took the scenic
tour through the Limestone Jags of the White Mountains National
Recreation Area. As our plane cleared the crest of a nearby hill,
Winston turned and pointed to the right. Atop barren tundra
mountaintops were ghostly limestone jags and ledges jutting out of
the ridgetops like obelisks commemorating a bygone era. Surprise
overwhelmed me. I hadn't known such unique geological forma-
tions and such attractive wilderness areas were so close to Fairbanks. We also flew over limestone caves, massive rock pinnacles,
cliffs, cold springs and underground streams. And at the end of this
whirlwind tour, complete with sightings of Dall sheep, we arrived at
Beaver Creek, all within an hour's flight time.

Beaver Creek originates at the confluence of Bear and Champion
creeks in the eastern portion of the one million-acre White Mountains National Recreation Area. In 1980, Congress designated 127
miles of Beaver Creek, starting from its beginnings at the
confluence of Bear and Champion creeks, as part of the National
Wild and Scenic River system. The national wild river portion of
Beaver Creek is within the boundaries of the White Mountains
National Recreation Area. It would also be our fishing destination
for the day.

65

Access to Upper Beaver Creek is via wheeled aircraft. Water levels dictate the number and location of landing areas. Because most gravel bars are small, anglers should keep gear to a minimum of 40 pounds per person, plus raft.

Opposite page: Beaver Creek grayling are old, slow growing fish that rarely exceed 14 inches, but are extremely plentiful. They relish high-floating, bushy dry flies.

Our pilot landed the Helio Courier on a long, sun-bleached gravel bar. We quickly unloaded our gear, and told him to pick us up in eight hours at a strip several miles downstream.

We took turns at the foot pump, and soon the inflatable took shape. Within minutes we were floating down Beaver Creek.

The water of Beaver Creek is exceptionally clear. The first 20 miles of the river drops in elevation about eight feet per mile. The water runs in a narrow channel 50 feet wide and one to three feet deep. Rafts and canoes can float this part throughout the summer, although there are occasional shallow riffles that require dragging the craft. As we floated along, I noticed an absence of footprints, trash or any indication of human encroachment. This was a special treat, especially having spent a week in the Nome area, where so called "wilderness" rivers were littered with trash, cut trees and footprints.

We did little raft dragging the first mile. Grayling fishing was slow at first, then picked up to nearly a fish a cast. These weren't husky Ugashik-size fish, but respectable grayling in the 10 to 14-inch category. They did exhibit some of the most beautiful dorsal fins I've seen on grayling anywhere in the state.

"Beaver Creek contains a good population of grayling," Winston said as we walked to a side pool. "It also contains salmon and sheefish, but we have limited data available on these species. For the last two years, the Bureau of Land Management has been monitoring and taking inventory of the fish in Beaver Creek. We've conducted water quality surveys, along with aerial reconnaissances and field observations of not only grayling, but wildlife and plant life."

According to a recent survey provided to me earlier by Sharon

Durgan Wilson, I discovered some interesting statistics on the Beaver Creek fishery.

Sampling by hook and line from June 20 to 27 of that year, the biologists caught 181 grayling. Thirty-six percent were males, and 64 percent females. They ranged from 5.5 to 14.5 inches in fork length, and one to 18 ounces in weight. The biologists sampled each index site for one hour, and randomly sampled the areas between each site for a total of five hours. Catch rate was 15.1 fish per hour—demonstrating that your chances of action in this fishery are indeed, excellent, as I was finding out.

The Bureau of Land Management is responsible for fisheries habitat on federal land that it manages. To gauge the quality of the habitat, fisheries biologists monitor numbers of fish, general condition, etc. They have developed a formula that results in a "K factor"—the relationship of the length and weight of the fish. The weight of the fish varies with the cube of its length, provided the shape and specific gravity remain the same. Generally, a K factor above 1.0 reflects good condition or well-being. The K factor also indicates the suitability of an environment for fish. Judging from test results, Beaver Creek is an excellent environment for grayling. Of the six established index sites, four contained fish with K factors from 1.0 to 1.3, two sites produced fish with K factors of .94 and .96. At the seventh index site at river mile 111, no fish were captured because of shallow water and few pools.

Scales were taken and age class determinations were made for 55 grayling. The fish ranged from two-year-olds measuring 5.5 inches in length to nine-year-olds measuring 14.3 inches long. Seventy-three percent of the fish caught were between five and seven years old.

Beaver Creek is a slow, meandering waterway that also serves as home to caribou, moose and bear, as well as sheep at higher elevations. Salmon, pike and whitefish are found in lesser numbers in the lower drainage.

Opposite page: Limestone jags thrust out of the tundra mountaintops surrounding Beaver Creek. Geologists have found caves and fossils in the area.

Biologists implanted radio tags in the body cavities of two grayling in the fall, and monitored them through spring. It took 24 days after tagging for the fish to travel 30 miles downstream to the overwintering area about one mile below the confluence of Trail and Beaver creeks. Both fish were still in the overwintering site on May 10 when ice was covering most of Trail Creek, but radio signals from the tags were weak or barely discernible. That was the last recorded location of the fish, so it is not known where they migrated to spawn.

Grayling have been prolific in Beaver Creek for many years; salmon sightings have been less frequent. Only kings and chums seem to be represented in Beaver Creek, and there is no true picture of salmon population size. Upper Beaver Creek is not considered to be a salmon spawning stream of any consequence due to low and inconsistent water flows, and the substrate of lower Beaver Creek contains too much silt for good spawning grounds.

Salmon have been seen in portions of the drainage. In late July, chum salmon have been spotted 41 miles above Victoria Creek. Chinook salmon can be found in the area during the same time period. Beaver Creek is a modest salmon fishery awaiting to be discovered.

Other fish in Beaver Creek include northern pike, burbot, whitefish, sheefish, slimy sculpins and long-nose suckers. Northern pike are rare, although their numbers increase in the downstream areas as the creek nears the Yukon Flats. Burbot, which makes a great poor man's lobster, hold in deep pools in the river, although they may move into the shallows to feed at night. They don't move around much until spawning time in January or February, when they congregate in moderately shallow water. Round whitefish are resident in Beaver Creek, migrating only to the gravely shallows of the river to spawn in late September through October.

Inconnu, or sheefish, are occasionally caught in Beaver Creek. They are small fish, rarely exceeding 15 pounds. The fish may come from the upper Yukon River, but little is known about sheefish in this watershed.

We had caught over 20 grayling from one stretch of riffles located below a rugged rock cliff face before Winston, Adela and I shoved off to explore new fishing waters.

While floating down the creek, the three of us fished, and on many occasions had three fish on at once. In one stretch, placing the lure in the water wasn't necessary to catch a grayling. Dangling a fly or lure six inches above the surface enticed several fish to leap out of the water in unison and grab the fly. Along a rocky, limestone shoreline, we watched as many as eight grayling charge after the fly we placed on the water.

The float was an idyl of blue skies, fishing adventure and good company. Best of all, we didn't observe a single boat or angler the entire day. As we relaxed while drifting through the fishless stretches, Winston pointed out several birds of prey and the various plant communities that make up this region.

Eight hours passed quickly. At the pull-out point, Adela snapped photos while I made a few last casts, dropping a Blue Dun at the edge of a current breakline along the far shore. Grayling after grayling rose with a splash, with several jumping out of the water and coming down head-first on the fly.

We heard the drone of the plane, and I reluctantly reeled in the fly line and headed toward shore. I had felt good about the entire day, a feeling that I'm sure Winston and Adela also shared. We didn't kill a single fish, and I was glad of it.

Proposed recreational development of the White Mountains National Recreation Area, which includes increased road access, trails, overnight camping areas, picnic areas and river access to Beaver Creek, will undoubtedly increase recreational use and fishing activity in this area. Increasing fishing pressure may lead to greater harvest of grayling and impact the population of older age classes or spawning adult fish. Unless ADF&G implements a catch and release policy for this area, I'm sure the quality of fishing we experienced will be lost. And that's a shame. An area so wild and scenic deserves the respect of a catch and release fishery.

In the meantime, take time this summer to explore the majesty of the White Mountains National Recreation Area, and a float trip down Beaver Creek. It's a quiet type of adventure that leaves the soul refreshed and provides a greater appreciation of the Alaska outdoors, without the crowds.

Planning Your Trip

WHEN TO GO

Grayling fishing on Beaver Creek is good from June through September. Anglers have over 20 hours of daylight during June and early July. Waters are often muddy from spring run-off the first half of June, but clear up by month's end.

WHAT TO TAKE

A 2 or 4-weight rod is most effective on Beaver Creek grayling. They are not the least bit hesitant about rising to dry flies. Bivisibles, gnats, Wulffs, stoneflies, mayflies and Adams all worked equally well during our float. In the deeper pools, hare's ear, caddis nymph and leech patterns worked best. A size 8 polar shrimp also worked exceptionally well. We fished this with a 10-foot sink tip.

HOW TO GET THERE

To reach Beaver Creek by road, drive 56 miles north from Fairbanks on the Steese Highway. The road is paved from Fairbanks to mile 44; the rest of the road is gravel. Turn left at U.S. Creek Road, a gravel road that has been improved since it was first cut by local gold miners. A two-wheel drive vehicle will get you to Nome Creek, but you will need a four-wheel drive vehicle to continue along Nome Creek to Moose Creek.

After the first 20 miles, the river channel doubles its width, from 75 to 150 feet, in the next 80 miles. It averages from two to four feet deep, and the river gradient continues to drop about eight feet per mile. In the first half of this section, Beaver Creek is fed by Trail, Wickersham and Fossil creeks. At several locations, Beaver Creek separates into two main channels that flow separately for up to a mile. The stream substrate is a mixture of small stones, pebbles and sand, and there are many exposed gravel bars.

Willow, Sheep and Warren creeks enter Beaver Creek between 50 and 99 miles downstream from the headquarters. The stream continues to drop at the same rate as it flows through low-lying hills in this section.

For the last 27 miles of the national wild river portion, Beaver Creek slows as the gradient gradually reduces to about two feet per mile. River channel widths increase up to 150 feet, with an average water depth of two to six feet, and overall water quality remains excellent. Victoria Creek joins Beaver Creek in this section, 111 miles from the beginning. The river substrate is predominantly a mixture of gravels and sand, but it also contains more silt than the first 100 river miles. Most floaters arrange to be picked up by aircraft from the gravel bars in this area, which are larger and wider and more frequent than upstream.

Beaver Creek flows into the marshy flatlands of the Yukon Flats

National Wildlife Refuge 127 miles from its beginning, continuing another 176 miles before it dumps into the Yukon River.

An alternate method of access is to charter a flight to a convenient gravel bar on Beaver Creek.

Super Cub access to Beaver Creek is an inexpensive way to enjoy this area. Carrying capacity is one passenger and gear weighing no more than 500 pounds, however, limiting baggage weight to 60 to 150 pounds is recommended. Check with the air charter pilot. Cost is approximately $130 per hour, which includes the plane's return flight to Fairbanks, so plan on 40 minutes to 1.5 hours, depending on destination.

A Helio-Courier will carry 800 pounds a load, and will cost about $300 per trip. For large groups, rent an Otter. This heavy-duty, single-engine plane will carry 2,200 pounds and cost $415 per trip.

Most river travelers have an airplane pick them up from the gravel bars around Victoria Creek at river mile 176, about a one-week float trip from Nome Creek. Some continue their float down to the Yukon River and take out at the bridge. This 176-mile segment will take an additional week due to slow-moving water. The water is deep enough for a shallow-draft motorized boat.

River travelers can put in at Nome Creek, then float a minimum of two days to reach Beaver Creek. If the water is low, you will have to drag your raft or canoe. If it is high, there are many sharp turns, compressed water and sweepers ready to tip you over. Check with the BLM office, Steese/White Mountains District, for water conditions before you depart by calling (907) 474-2350.

WHERE TO STAY

This is a do-it-yourself, wilderness adventure, which means taking all camping and travel gear.

WHO TO CONTACT

For a listing of guides, outfitters and do-it-yourself services, turn to page 208, "Free Information to Plan Your Trip."

7 Adventure

A Kenai king takes to the air for this party of driftboat anglers.

The Kenai: River of Trophy Kings

THE KENAI ISN'T THE LONGEST RIVER IN ALASKA, nor does she have a sweet bouquet typical of water found in remote wilderness streams, the type that soothes a parched throat with every swallow. No, the Kenai River has qualities that transcend beyond those of other watersheds.

She is the reigning queen in a realm of princely streams and rivers, the epitome of power, elegance and grandeur. When you first gaze upon her, don't shrink back from her royalty. Rather, experience her openly with your senses. Listen to her currents hiss with energy as she flows by, and feel her riffles tug untiringly at your legs. Gaze into the ethereal glow of her turquoise-green current—the result of light refracting off microscopic particles of silt—and wonder in awe as to her very beginnings.

To view the source of the river's power, don't look into her depths. Rather, scan the spire-studded horizon. There, massive glaciers and icefields, Pleistocene Era sculptors of valley and mountain that span as far as the eye can see, give birth to this aqueous marvel. Yet, the icefields are a testimonial to the adage

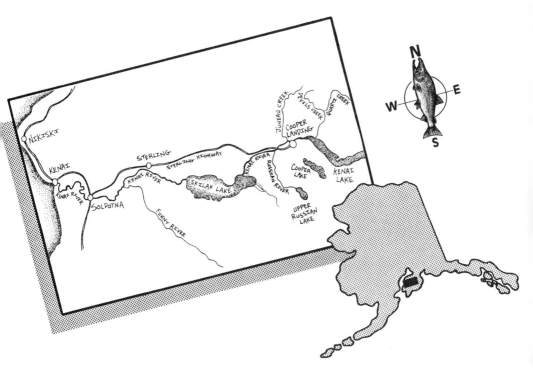

that "greatness begets greatness," even through death.

The death comes each summer, as the sun's rays blast the Kenai's patriarchal glaciers, reducing their towering, rough-hewn forms to bland ribbons of silt-laden water. Yet through this death, there is life. The resulting ice-melt creeks are the intricate chromosomes of Nature and icefield. They intertwine down mountain and across swamp and tundra, extracting the very essence of the land to form the genetic blueprint of the Kenai River. As the river takes form, larger creeks and streams are like umbilical cords that provide additional sustenance. In the womb of this land, the river grows in size and strength. After many miles and days, the infant river gradually transforms into a robust matriarch, giving life and refuge to all that cling to her, especially her fish species.

Anglers have only recently come to appreciate that as the glaciers impart their greatness upon the Kenai, so does the Kenai pass on this quality to her own. While the river has many children in the forms of trout, char and salmon, her most popular son is the Kenai king, the largest strain of salmon in the world.

Each year, thousands of Kenai kings return to the river, matriarchates that have lived through four to seven years of battle and survival on the high seas. Words can't aptly describe these Goliaths of the sportfishing realm. They rule by their actions and appearances. Fifty and 60 pounders are common, with numerous 70 and 80 pounders caught each year. In 1985, the new, all-tackle world

Guide Joe Conners takes a pair of needlenose pliers to release a Kenai king caught by angler Alan Kimura. The fish took a red and chartreuse Spin-N-Glo.

Opposite page: Adela Batin releases a 45-pound-plus Kenai River king salmon. This quality king fishery will continue only when sport and commercial fishermen acknowledge the importance of this unique strain of salmon, and restrict their catches accordingly.

record for a king salmon was broken with a 97.4-pound behemoth. Set netters claimed to have found spawned-out kings that could have weighed well over 100 pounds.

Yet the Kenai is not one to give up her salmon treasures easily. The water is turbid, limiting visibility. The current is swift and treacherous to those unfamiliar with it. As for fishing, many techniques used in catching kings in clear-water rivers are ineffective on the Kenai. They often require modification, before salmon can be put into the boat. Chances are, if you want a big king, you'll fail if you go it alone. Nearly 60 percent of all kings caught on the Kenai are by anglers fishing with a guide.

There are guides who can fish the Kenai, and there are guides who understand the Kenai. Joe Conners is one of the few that can do both. Conners owns Big Sky Charter, a fish camp specializing in catching both the great Kenai king, chunky rainbow trout and the river's aristocratic silver salmon.

Conners has fished the Kenai for over 20 years. He deciphers the river when she's temperamental and angry, and carefully harvests her goods when she's generous. Because of this philosophy, Conners is respected in the highly competitive world of Kenai fishing guides.

A guide that truly understands his water has an unshakable air of confidence about him. Conners is no exception. It was a bit past 7 a.m. on a June day when I pulled up to Conners camp located in Sterling. It was a clear, bright bluebird day, one that calls fishermen into action from across southcentral Alaska. And they heed the call in boats of all shapes and sizes, churning up the Kenai to their favorite fishing holes. We quickly joined the procession.

On the way to Conner's first fishing hole, I felt the anxiety of fishing the Kenai. Sure, it's crowded, and the shoreline is lined with people. But where else can you stand a fair to good chance of catching an all-tackle, world-record king salmon? Indeed, the Kenai not only produces big fish, but also plenty of them. Most king salmon rivers in Alaska have just one run of kings. The Kenai is one of the major streams that has two. The early run, starting in mid May and lasting through the first week in July, produces fish from the small, precocious jack salmon up to an average of 30 pounds, with increasingly more fish in recent years showing up in the 60 to 90-pound category. These fish tend to mill around the main river and nearby spawning tributaries for about 24 days. Expect these salmon to be chrome bright and full of spunk.

But the second-run fish are the true gladiators. Some call them soakers, lunkers, hogs and slabs. Whatever the appellation, second-run salmon enter the river as early as May, but are predominant in early to mid July, with spawning taking place after the season closure at month's end.

Evolution has had a hand in making the second-run Kenai king what it is today. In late spring, Kenai River tributaries have ample water from melting ice and snow. First-run kings can spawn safely in these streams. As water levels drop during mid-summer, these streams are mere trickles. This low water would subject second-run kings to injury or predation. Thus, biologists theorize, it's possible that the large size of second-run kings is the direct result of coping with the rigors of spawning in the Kenai's swift, main current.

Kenai kings are normally six-year fish, yet exhibit an atypical behavior for spending an extra year at sea. There they gorge themselves on herring and other baitfish. According to a recent report by the Alaska Department of Fish and Game, 4.1 percent of early-run fish and 8.2 percent of the late run caught by anglers were seven years old. In some years, the incidence of seven-year-old fish increases dramatically. About 60 percent of both runs are six-year-old kings. The remaining fish consists of other age categories. Of course, this percentage varies from year to year.

Much of the fishing pressure on the Kenai is concentrated in the lower half of the river, and for good reason. Most of the second-run kings choose spawning beds from Mile 10 to 21. On the average, these fish are available to anglers for 12.8 days. But the guide who catches fish is one who's willing to move with the salmon. In normal currents, males travel the fastest; about 18 miles per day. Females travel about nine miles per day. According to the results of a preliminary study on Kenai kings conducted by the U.S. Fish and Wildlife Service, the salmon tend to migrate most during late afternoon and evening.

The upper Kenai offers excellent fishing for large rainbow trout. Only unmotorized driftboats are allowed. Anglers have the choice of fishing from the boat or fly fishing from various gravel bars and points. Ten to 15-pound 'bows are caught every year.

As we slowed to a stop, Conners explained how big kings relate to structure.

"Big kings are found primarily along their migration routes," he said. "On the Kenai, these will be channels and runs from 12 to 60 feet of the river bank. Vegetated islands are also good areas that provide cover for spawning or resting kings. Yet Kenai kings aren't always predictable."

There's a trick to hooking kings out of holes, slots, or at the head of riffles. For instance, many guides will fish for kings behind rocks. Smart guides like Conners fish for them ahead of rocks. In most cases, the water behind the rock is too turbulent for kings, yet suitable for Dolly Varden and rainbow trout.

As I pondered Conners' comments, it dawned on me that successful Kenai king anglers and guides have several things in common. They spend plenty of time on the water, they know the habits of the fish, and they use the right tackle. However, specific knowledge of the Kenai is also important for consistent success.

The choice of fishing lure and technique greatly depends on several factors. In a strong current, it's necessary to use a deep-diving plug. In deep water, back-bouncing a bait will take fish when all else fails. Conditions may change several times throughout the course of a day, so it's necessary to watch, and be prepared to change lures and tactics. Carefully judging the water conditions, I pulled out a black and red Spin-N-Glo, one of my favorite color combos for bright light conditions.

Before I rigged up, I immediately took the water temperature: 45 degrees. At temperatures below 48 degrees, Conners believes a large, gaudy lure—such as a Spin-N-Glo/hootchie combo with a bright,

Because of the glacial turbidity of the Kenai, a salmon's visibility is greatly restricted. Large fluorescent plugs work best when fished from boats. Shore anglers hook fish by bottom bouncing drift lures as well as large spinners and spoons.

iridescent glob of salmon eggs attached—must be dangled in front of the fish to entice a strike. The fish will move only a short distance to intercept the lure. I reminded myself that the take would be very soft; that the salmon will merely open its mouth and gently close it on the lure. I also reminded myself to set the hook at the slightest hesitation in the movement of the lure.

With that in mind, I tied on a red and black Spin-N-Glo/hootchie combo complete with diving planer. I spooled out 30 yards of line, allowed the lure to dive, and proceeded to talk Kenai fishing techniques with Conners.

When fishing the early season, successful anglers anchor their boat and use a jet planer with a trailing Spin-N-Glo and hootchie combo in solid colors. Why solid colors? I believe early-run fish are subjected to the glitter of millions of in-migrating smelt during the first part of June. These salmon appear to become immune to flash.

Therefore, solid colors—especially fluorescent red, chartreuse and the Hi-Glo pearlescent finishes—seem to work best. You might also consider the metallic blues and greens. They don't exhibit the hard flash that is cast off by chrome, nickel or silver-plated lures.

Stay away from non-fluorescent colors because they lose their intensity in the turbid waters of the Kenai. Fluorescent-colored diving plugs such as the Storm Magnum Wiggle Warts backtrolled behind a boat also work good at this time. For the uninitiated, backtrolling is a technique where the boat is motored upstream at a speed slightly slower than the current. The result is that the boat slips very slowly downstream, enabling the angler to cover a lot of river-bottom but still tease the fish with a lure that remains in front of its nose for a considerable period of time.

Second-run fish require different techniques that will aggravate them into striking. Fluorescent colors appear to be most effective in doing this because a fish can see the lure bouncing toward it from upriver. Or, use colors with substantial contrast, such as black and fluorescent red.

The longer a Kenai king can see a lure coming—especially if it's heading right for the salmon's strike zone, an area that expands and contracts with water temperature and water clarity—the quicker an aggravation response builds. If conditions are right, the salmon strikes.

A bit of flash, either from a metallic surface, spinner blade, spoon or prism tape applied to the lure, is often effective in making the lure highly visible and enhancing the aggravation response. The flash principle works well on second-run Kenai kings, as the hooligan are usually gone from the river by early July.

Second-run fishing techniques vary with individual anglers and guides. While I favor backtrolling migration channels or holding areas with plugs, or jet-planing Spin-N-Glo hootchie combos, Conners adds another element: scent. I can't disagree. There is no denying the effectiveness of scent in one area: disguising human scent and attracting salmon.

By disguising the human or lure scent with a home-made or commercially prepared scent, I believe it is possible to have at least all bases covered when fishing for that 90-pounder; a fish that may have busted three lines since entering the river, and will probably bust two more before reaching its spawning grounds.

On the Kenai, I recommend using scent on all artificial lures, especially when eggs are inappropriate or illegal. My observations are that in heavily fished areas—and the Kenai receives over 100,000 man-hours of fishing pressure annually—additional scent added to the lure might help influence the salmon to strike, especially if the fish was hooked previously.

When fishing for Kenai kings, it's also imperative that you replace the original hooks on your lure with extra-strong singles, and epoxy the screw eyes into the plugs. Most importantly, however, make sure the hooks are sharp.

On Spin-N-Glo/hootchie combos, wire leaders are also a must as they take the most abuse from river bottom rocks and the teeth of a big king.

Indeed, the trick to catching a Kenai king is not only a thorough understanding of when and where to fish, but also understanding and implementing the smaller details that many anglers overlook.

Veteran Kenai king guide Dan Meyers battles a Kenai king to shore. After a 30-minute battle, he finally unhooked the fish and the salmon immediately shot out to deeper water. Recently, an angler fought a Kenai king for over 30 hours. The angler lost the fish at the net.

But once you've hooked "the king," you're in for a battle of a lifetime.

Keep in mind that kings are unpredictable once hooked. They may take to the air, sulk or exhibit fighting tactics that would make West Point stand up and take notice.

I remember boating through Big Eddy several years ago with friend Crazy Mike, a hopeless king addict. We drifted by a lone angler glued to the transom of his boat. He was attempting to control a freshly-hooked king. This is a common sight and wouldn't have warranted stopping. But the angler had kicked his foot up on the gunwale for more leverage, which meant a lunker fish.

When the king retaliated by nearly yanking the angler over the side of the boat, it became obvious this would be a three-man operation. The next two hours and several miles downriver were charged with the electricity that is Kenai king fishing. This red-hued, king salmon buck used every inch of the river. He charted a crash course—his back breaking the surface—through fishing lines, around rocks and through sweepers (trees hanging out horizontally from the bank and washed by the current).

Several times the fish sounded for the bottom in heavy current, refusing to budge. Once it did move, the salmon streaked downstream, splitting 100 yards of current in 10 seconds.

The angler, a middle-aged, East Coast native, was beginning to feel the effects of the battle. His initial whoops and hollers had long since stopped, and the butts from several cigarettes littered the deck. He continued to puff away wildly as he grunted the fish near the boat.

Gerry Cleary with a 61-pound king salmon he caught while fishing the second run of kings that enter the river in mid July. Guided anglers outfish unguided anglers by at least three to one.

A giant, tooth-lined maw soon broke the water's surface. Seeing that the hooks were nearly straightened and about to pull out, Mike—who had jumped aboard the angler's boat earlier with our large net—made a jab at the fish.

The salmon barely fit into the net.

As Mike muscled the fish over the side, the bottom of the net suddenly burst. The thrashing king slammed down on the boat's railing. It hung there for what seemed like an eternity.

To this day, I believe it was the force of the angler's fearful scream that made the salmon fall back into the boat.

The king weighed in at 73 pounds, much to the delight of the easterner who seemed to have suffered a facial stroke—he never stopped smiling for the remainder of the day.

But the Kenai is much more than a big salmon river. It is one of the best, big river rainbow fisheries in the region. Those who don't know how to fish the Kenai will scoff, but pay no heed to these skeptics. Guides like Conners personally hook Dolly Varden and rainbow trout from eight to 12 pounds each autumn on both flies and spinning tackle. Another guide, Dan Meyers of Kenai, has helped anglers land slab-sided bows in the 15 to 20-pound range. These are more than flukes. They are an indication that the Kenai is a fishery with plenty to offer.

And last but not least, don't forget the huge runs of sockeye salmon. In recent years, as many as 100,000 per day have entered the river, prompting ADF&G to open up dip net fisheries to harvest the excess fish. But catch your sockeye on a fly rod, and you won't be disappointed.

However, the Kenai fishery is far from being impervious to destruction. Problems with subsistence use, set netters and heavy fishing pressure have all directly impacted the king runs over the years. Development of shoreline critical to salmon rearing has land managers worried about the future of these salmon runs. These problems are being addressed individually, and hopefully, progress in resolving the conflicts is on the horizon. For too long, the Kenai River king run has been a meat-oriented fishery. It's time for a change.

With plenty to think about from our discussion on the Kenai, we decided to take a coffee break, and Joe began to pull into shore.

Just as I was about to lift the steaming brew to my lips, I saw friend Alan Kimura's rod tip slam down and out, and it stayed down! He responded with a solid hookset, and the battle was on. The fish was strong, but Alan buried the butt in his mid section and hung tight.

A Kenai king deserves the title, "heavyweight sportfish champ of Alaska." This salmon uses both its weight and the Kenai's swift current to wear down equipment and angler. And after 20 minutes of battle, Alan's fish was succeeding in doing just that. The king had taken us a half-mile downriver, and we had yet to see it. Finally, after another five minutes of battle, the fish jumped, shaking itself wildly, as if annoyed by this miniscule piece of wire in its jaw. The king then surged upriver while we drifted downriver.

For the next 10 minutes, Alan applied all the pressure that 25-pound-test would allow. Finally, the fish surfaced. It was an absolute beauty, newly arrived from the ocean, probably on the morning tide. Minutes later, Joe eased the fish into the net and pulled it to the boat's side.

"It'll go 35 pounds. Want to keep it?"

"Let it go," Alan replied. "I'll catch a bigger one next drift."

My records show that throughout the past 17 years, I've caught and released my share of Kenai king salmon. Yet, you'd think that anglers, myself included, would get used to the punishment these fish dish out. But we don't. I guess if we did, it wouldn't be Kenai king fishing.

Planning Your Trip

WHEN TO GO

For big kings, plan on fishing in July, the later the better. In recent years, however, big kings have been caught as early as May and June. Rainbow fishing is fair to good all summer, especially in the upper stretches, however, the largest fish are taken in August, September and October.

WHAT TO TAKE

For big kings, use a 7 to 8 1/2-foot medium-heavy action graphite or equivalent rod with a limber tip and stiff spine. It should balance with an Ambassadeur 7000 filled with 25 to 40-pound test line. Due to the turbid glacial water, high-visibility lines are a must when fishing the Kenai. For bottom bouncing, you'll need two to three-foot black, plastic-coated wire leaders rated 40-pound test. Take along a flat file and stone to sharpen hooks; sliding sinker sleeves, and a selection of one-half to three-ounce teardrop sinkers and wire twist-ons, for attaching the weight to the sleeve.

A popular lure is a clown pattern (chartreuse with red dots) Spin-N-Glo with a fluorescent orange hootchie tail. Other good colors include white and black (Snoopy), metallic silver and fluorescent orange, peach, and fluorescent red. Use a series of red plastic beads, Okies or Lil' Corkies for bearings and as additional attractors. Depending on what current regulations will allow, rig the lure with one or two single 6/0 extra-strong steel hooks. Fish the Spin-N-Glo/hootchie with either a sliding sinker or a Jet Planer.

As for plugs, Storm Magnum Wiggle Warts in metallic gold, silver, chartreuse, fluorescent orange or any combination of the above colors are the most popular. Some guides carry several cans of fluorescent spray paint and create color combinations necessary to catch fish.

Most guides offer complete equipment and lures. You need to bring raingear and a jacket. Hip boots or rubber boots are preferred, but not necessary.

HOW TO GET THERE

The Kenai River is located about 150 miles south of Anchorage. Access is by road or scheduled air service.

WHERE TO STAY

Many charter operators with day trips offer package deals on accommodations which are less expensive than regular motel rates. Choose one that offers meals and accommodations at a price cheaper than what you can purchase them separately in Kenai or Soldotna. Numerous campgrounds are available on the Kenai Peninsula; however, these book quickly from June through August.

APPROXIMATE COSTS

A day fishing trip on the Kenai runs from $150 to $250 per day, the latter includes accommodations and meals.

WHO TO CONTACT

For a listing of guides, outfitters and do-it-yourself services, turn to page 208, "Free Information To Plan Your Trip."

8 Adventure

Some of the finest fly fishing for lake trout, char and grayling is available on Walker Lake, which is surrounded by glacial remnants from the last Great Ice Age.

Fishing in the Land of Midnight Fire

THROUGHOUT ALASKA, there are waters that offer panoramic beauty, and scores that provide fish-after-fish action and excitement. Still others offer the tranquility of big fish in mountain solitude. In the heart of the Brooks Range, you'll find that Walker Lake offers all these attributes, and something more: sportfishing drama unique to this region of the world.

During that day in mid June, as I have done so often in the past, I succumbed to the sportfishing passions that Walker so readily nurtures. I forgot about time, an easy thing to do when fishing in the Land of the Midnight Sun. The melancholy swirls of warm air that had brushed my face for over 19 hours quickly lost their soothing caress in the cool twilight. I looked at my watch. It was a few minutes before midnight, and the sun was rapidly disappearing behind the massive spires of the Brooks Range.

The mountaintops acted as giant candle snuffers, extinguishing the last rays of visible light. Nearby clouds metamorphosed from cottonball white to a metal-gray. Twilight gained strength in the absence of sunlight, prompting me to hunker into my boat seat for

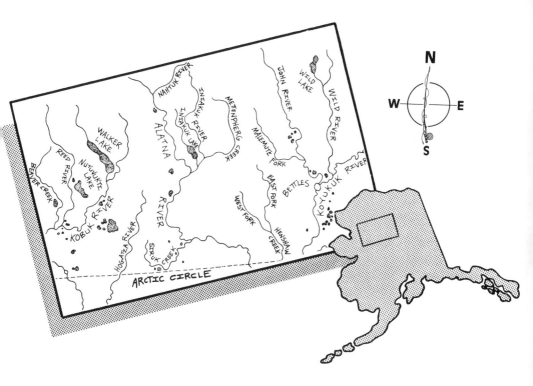

warmth and to watch the evening magic at work.

Slowly, the chill ushered in a quiet that hushed life in this alpine environment. Ghostly apparitions of mist rose from the lake's mirrored surface, their slim, feathery plumes dancing and sliding across a nearby bay. The encroaching shadows of towering, shoreline mountains devoured the sun-drenched shoreline and slid out onto the lake, engulfing it in a somber blue shroud.

It was the summer equinox in the Brooks Range, when total darkness is a stranger, and the life span of twilight is but a few heartbeats. Suddenly, a single sunburst pierced the northeastern sky, searing it in an aura of orange. Like moths being consumed in flames, shadows weakened and fell. The increasing rays of light were a midnight fire in the northern sky, igniting mountain peaks and valleys, basking all life with its warm glow. A new day was born.

After such a spectacle, fishing almost seemed anti-climatic, I thought to myself. But I decided to indulge anyway.

I motored to shore to pick up my wife, Adela, and we moved out 100 yards to the edge of a weed-covered drop-off. Adela caught several lake trout before I finally hooked a respectable 12-pounder.

The battle was fun, until I saw a shape coming up the drop-off from deep water. In disbelief, I unconsciously dropped my rod tip.

The fish was a huge lake trout, and it was homing in on the fish I was battling.

One of the thrills of fishing the Brooks Range in late June is watching the sun dip toward the horizon at midnight, then rise again, following a circular path in the northern sky. Anglers often lose track of time in the plentitude of daylight.

I watched the 20-pound-plus invader bite at the lure hanging from my fish's mouth. I couldn't speak. Rather, I grunted something to gain Adela's attention. She caught one glance of the fish, and retrieved her line at high speed. I pulled up as much as I dared on my light-action rod, hoping to save my fish from certain demise. I also hoped to keep the laker's interest until Adela could cast to it. The 20-pounder, however, kept striking at the lure in the fish's mouth. Then, in what seemed to be an act of frustration, it attacked the fish itself, sinking its toothy maw around its head.

Adela dropped her lure into the water, and immediately the 20-pounder darted over, made a swipe at the lure, and swam back to chomp on my fish again.

"Flutter it along the bottom!" I screeched, excitement getting the better of me.

She dropped the jig to the bottom, and worked it slowly, kicking up clouds of silt. The fish darted over and sucked in her jig. Adela exhaled a shout of excitement as her medium-action rod doubled over under the weight of the fish.

The battle lasted 20 seconds before the line went slack. The hook simply cut out of the fish.

Obviously disappointed, Adela looked at her lure, smiled in the encompassing brightness of the midnight fire, and said, "That fish was the size of a full-grown beaver, with a potbelly to match."

This is but one of many fond memories I have of fishing Walker Lake, located in the heart of the Brooks Range in northcentral Alaska. There are several reasons why it is one of my favorite fishing spots. One is limitless scenery. The impressive Arrigetch Peaks line the far horizon. Huge rockslides of quartz and other

Nick Jennings photographs a large lake trout that Adela Batin eventually brought to the boat and released. Walker Lake is extremely clear down to at least 50 feet, and anglers often delight in watching lake trout and char grab their lures.

minerals jut out of alder and stone mountainsides. And high above the clouds, glacially carved peaks, cirques and massive amphitheaters exhibit an awesome, foreboding personality all their own.

Remoteness is another reason. Don't expect the lake to be whipped to a froth from jet boaters and water skiers. Walker Lake is located inside the Gates of the Arctic National Park, which is an area larger than Massachusetts, Delaware and Rhode Island combined. Access to the park is by float plane only, with the nearest road more than 100 miles to the east, and the city of Fairbanks 250 miles to the south.

Perhaps best of all, Walker Lake offers excellent fishing for lake trout, arctic char and grayling. Lakers range from six to 12 pounds, with trophy fish going well over the 20-pound mark. Arctic char range between five to 15 pounds. And there's an abundance of arctic grayling in the 16 to 18-inch class. In other nearby lakes and rivers, northern pike, burbot and chum salmon are also available.

Motoring the boat back to the lodge, we found Bud Helmericks leaning against an overturned boat, watching the midnight sun gaining strength. Bud, and his wife, Martha, own the only private land on Walker Lake, which is surrounded by national park. There, they have built a home and lodge. We told Bud of our encounter with the "beaver fish" and he shook his head.

"Luckily it wasn't the Walker Lake Monster," he replied. "One of the carpenters over at the lodge has been pursuing it for years. He claims the fish will go an easy 55 pounds. When he's here in the spring, you can often find him out trolling the deepest part of the lake with deep-sea tackle and a lure as big as my hand."

With that said, we were enthusiastic about fishing again, but it

Will and Deb Tinnesand admire this arctic char caught on a mid June excursion to Walker Lake. The two had extremely good success with a white twister tail and fluorescent red leadhead bounced along bottom.

Opposite page: Adela Batin discovers that fishing for lake trout on Walker Lake is best from mid June to mid July. Numbers of large fish are caught near shore.

would have to keep until later. It was getting late and we needed sleep. Besides, our arms and wrists were worn out from battles with headstrong lake trout and char.

The next morning, we motored down the lake to a secret spot where Bud said large char could be found. It didn't take more than a few minutes of jigging before I set the hook into a head-shaking char. I peered over the side of the boat and caught sight of the fish, battling it out in 40 feet of mountain-pure water.

As I slowly pumped the fish to the surface, its oranges and golds dazzled in reflective brilliance in the mid morning sun. Large, pink spots shined like jewels in a gold crown of miniature scales as the fish was brought to hand and carefully released. Adela was busy playing an 11-pound laker, which was etched with green and gold vermiculations. I savored every minute of the fishing in this locale. Adela eased the hook out of her trout. The fish tossed a mean-lookin' glance at her, snapped its jaws several times, and shot back down into the depths.

"I have a feeling you disturbed that fish from doing something important," I said, before setting the hook into another char.

"I'm just glad I'm not a fish swimming around in this lake," she replied, rubbing her fighting arm. "Even the small fish we caught have spunk. But these big ones are bundles of dynamite, to say the least."

Later that day, we observed schools of lake trout hovering over an underwater island we had found earlier. They finned slowly back and forth, holding along the island's structural breakline...that is, until Adela buzzed her lure above them. Several fish charged the lure, with a spunky eight-pounder grabbing and ingesting the jig

90

first. After a short tussle, Adela returned the fish to the water. We caught and released a few more lake trout before the school swam into the depths and disappeared.

Adela and I spent the next morning catching more lakers, char and grayling. We didn't keep count of how many we caught each day of the trip. This far north, days have neither beginning nor end, except for the illuminating glow or "fire" that comes immediately after midnight. We actively pursued the "Walker Lake Monster," but didn't connect. But it didn't matter. Just being in the area was cause to rejoice in being alive. And fishing, whether we caught one or 100 fish, was a means to celebrate this awareness.

For scenic wonder, superb lake fishing, and a chance to explore one of the most spectacular mountain ranges in the state, Walker Lake in mid June has no equal anywhere in the northcountry. But don't take my word for it. See for yourself.

Planning Your Trip

WHEN TO GO
Mid to late June is an ideal time to visit Walker Lake and Gates of the Arctic National Park. The fishing is spectacular, you'll see the midnight sun, and the weather is sunny with little rain.

WHAT TO TAKE
For a do-it-yourselfer, standard overnight camping gear, bug dope, inflatable boat, oars, and food. Take plenty of sunscreen, as well as long sleeve shirts to help protect against sunburn and mosquitoes. Take lots of insect repellent. Sunglasses are a must, as is a cap with visor.

Fly gear should consist of a 400-grain shooting head and running line for fishing for lake trout and char along the drop-offs, and a lighter 4-weight for the grayling around the lakeshore and outlet. Spin and level-wind anglers should use one-ounce flashy silver spoons, jigs and Storm Wiggle Warts in gold and silver. A downrigger and graph unit will help pinpoint fish schools.

HOW TO GET THERE
Take a commercial flight to Bettles, and charter to Walker Lake. For larger groups, it may be economical to charter directly from Fairbanks.

WHERE TO STAY
Pitch camp on a gravel bar at lake's outlet or inlet, or near any of the tributary streams. Camping permits are required from the National Park Service.

WHO TO CONTACT
For a listing of guides, outfitters and do-it-yourself services, turn to page 208, "Free Information To Plan Your Trip."

9 Adventure

Even in mid summer, the mountains of the Aleutian Range, just north of Iliamna, remain snow and glacier covered.

The Allure of Iliamna

UNLIKE THE STALE, SMOGGY WIND commonly found in big cities, the strong breeze blowing off Alaska's Ugashik Lake last summer was especially invigorating. Its nippy essence penetrated my skin, leaving me with an exhilarating feeling of having just traveled over alpine glaciers, along endless miles of snow-fed tundra, and through the dark fissures of volcanoes that have died long ago. Yet, I intuitively sensed another presence, one that caused my nerve endings to tingle and my stomach to fall into that bottomless abyss of anticipatory excitement.

I didn't have to wait long for the confrontation. Large schools of robust arctic char cruised out of the dark depths of Ugashik into water so clear I could see the bottom of a twenty-foot pool. The fish, not a one under eight pounds, were on the prowl. And from the looks of their husky, bronze-colored flanks, they were not the least bit particular about feeding.

In seeming defiance, the nearest char grabbed my flutter spoon several times, as if daring me to set the hook. I was mesmerized by the scene, and the char would have swam away in disinterest if it weren't for my hook-setting reflexes being on autopilot. The fight was on.

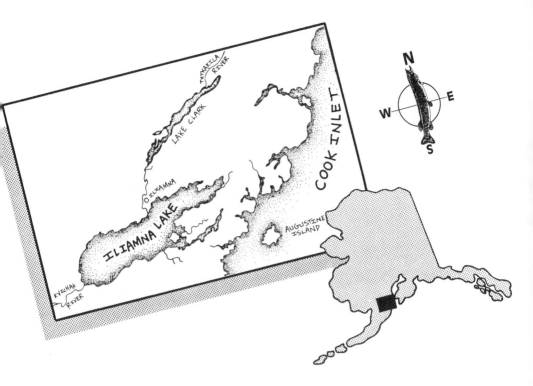

I watched the frenzy that took place 25 feet below the surface with wide-eyed astonishment. The char rolled like an errant cement mixer, twisting so violently that it collided into the sandy bottom several times. Other char nearby darted around in a frenzy, like sharks moving in on a kill.

"Don't put your hand in the water to tail that fish," my fishing partner, Adela, commented. "You may not get it back."

As it turned out, I lost both lure and fish. The char sizzled to the boat's bow and bounced the four-pound mono off the anchor chain. To complicate matters, the rolling whitecaps on Ugashik were increasing in strength, making it difficult to retie a proper knot.

When the weather speaks in a wilderness environment, it's the survivors who listen and obey, despite the quality of fishing taking place. Our guide, Will Kitsos, motored us back to shore. We would try our luck fishing the short, gravel stream connecting Upper and Lower Ugashik.

We rigged our fly rods, tied on six-foot leaders and pink egg patterns favored by Dolly Varden. Walking up the well-traveled bear trails that meandered along the stream's edge, we observed numerous crimson-colored sockeyes. With two or more to each redd, the salmon resembled British soldiers guarding their post. And waiting behind them, like hooligans about to commit foul play, were large Dolly Varden char. Long and silvery, they finned

95

Guide Will Kitsos is pleased with this October rainbow he caught while drift fishing the Newhalen River. Fly fisherman do equally well fishing egg patterns, orange roe crystal bullets and zonkers in the side pools and eddies.

patiently in the current, waiting to rob recently filled redds. The smaller char, however, were scattered throughout the stream. They intercepted free-floating salmon eggs with the swiftness and precision of purse snatchers.

I false cast the egg-fly into position, dropped it lightly at the head of a side riffle, and allowed it to sink. A sizable wake knifed out from the gravel bank. The water boiled as a Dolly struck with all-out aggression.

During the five-minute battle, a sockeye, seemingly infuriated by the twisting contortions of the 20-inch char, veered away from its redd and started to chomp on my fish's tail. The char began jumping with renewed vigor, and escaped serious injury from the salmon's half-inch long spawning teeth. I quickly brought the char to hand, and released it. The features of its metallic blue back, pink dots and white tipped fins faded from view as the fish moved upstream.

At days end, we had caught numerous grayling, 27 char, 17 sockeye and five silver salmon, all from a half-mile stretch of creek that emptied into the lake.

Unusual? Not really. We were fishing within flying distance of the Iliamna Lake area, which many anglers consider the epitome of Alaska sportfishing. In many cases, the appellation is justified.

Size is one reason. Covering more than 1,000 square miles, Lake Iliamna is Alaska's largest, and is fed or drained by numerous streams and tributaries, which include the Kvichak River and its

Lake trout are plentiful in the Lake Clark drainage, concentrating near freshwater inlets, off rocky points and near spawning salmon. During early summer, anglers can spend hours hooking and releasing fish from 2 to 20 or more pounds.

tributaries and all drainages flowing into Iliamna and Six-Mile Lake. Close by are the Naknek, Egegik and Ugashik drainages.

Numbers of fish are another plus. Iliamna's sockeye salmon runs are awe-inspiring, with as many as 62 million fish returning annually to its myriad lakes and rivers. The Kvichak River alone is the largest producer of sockeye salmon in the world. And in even-numbered years, pink salmon are abundant to the point of being "aquatic pests," time after time striking flies meant for other species.

While flying back to the lodge, I pointed out a few of the highlights of this region to visiting Texans who fished with us that day.

"Perhaps the most exciting part of Iliamna is its trophy rainbow fishery," I said. "Iliamna is the heart of the Bristol Bay Wild Trout Zone. The native rainbows in this region are among the largest in North America. Iliamna rainbows reach 10 to 15 or more pounds. At times, the only way to distinguish them from the chunky shape of 10 to 12-pound salmon is by color: salmon are red, rainbows are silvery blue. The life history of these fast-growing fish is worth knowing. They live in rivers until age two or three. Then they migrate into lakes such as Iliamna to live. They do embark on seasonal migrations to tributary streams to spawn in the spring. In September, they return to those same streams to feed on salmon eggs and chew on salmon carcasses."

"Rainbow trout eat salmon carcasses?" one Texan asked in disbelief, his voice rising above the drone of the Beaver engine.

97

One of the thrills of fishing the Iliamna-Lake Clark region is having a float plane at your disposal to explore the myriad lake and stream fisheries concentrated in this region.

Opposite page: Tim Hagerty with a fly-caught silver salmon he hooked while on a daily fly-out fishing trip north of Iliamna.

"Sounds more like a catfish trait to me."

"You bet they do," I said. "I've seen smaller trout chew off bits of salmon, and feed on the scraps of salmon washed away from feeding gulls and mammals. That's why a flesh fly is so effective at this time of the year."

Even after a long day of fishing, I could see the Texans were anxious to fish again. I was getting jazzed myself. Our pilot, George, fueled our angling desire with a few more words.

"Trophy-size arctic grayling are plentiful throughout the Iliamna watershed," he said, "especially in Ugashik Narrows and points farther north. Pike, lake trout and whitefish are also abundant.

"What species we pursue first depends on customer preference, and what's available at the time and weather conditions," George said as he banked the plane over the Kvichak River. "We can fly anglers anywhere within a 200-square mile radius of Iliamna, which includes such trophy fish areas as far south as Ugashik, as far west as Bristol Bay, and as far north as the Mulchatna system. But much of the best fishing is done directly south of Iliamna, and on the Naknek, Kvichak and smaller streams and creeks, and in Katmai National Monument."

As we flew over the Kvichak River, we observed a half dozen float-equipped aircraft and their anglers nearby. Because Iliamna is a world-class fishery, anglers should not be fooled into believing this is a total wilderness fishery. Once remote locations are receiving more and more fishing pressure. Consequently, air charter pilots and lodges are working harder to put their anglers out of the crowds' reach. Those who work at it, either by hiking a bit farther upstream, flying farther afield, or braving the weather during the off-season months, can expect excellent fishing. Anglers can expect the most crowds during the peak of the king and coho season.

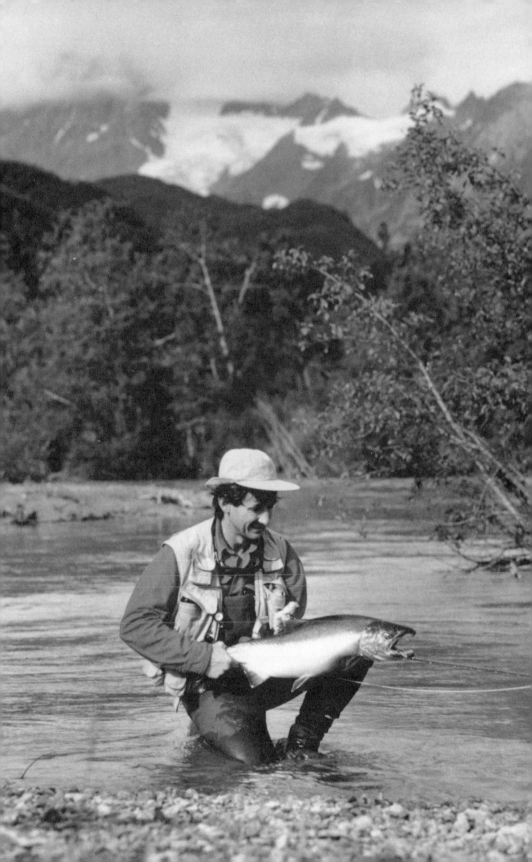

"Kings arrive in late June, and stay strong through the month of July," George said. "Pink, chum and sockeye are available in late June and all of July. Silvers are most plentiful in August. Rainbow are available in most all waters except Lake Clark and the Ugashik system. Arctic char, Dolly Varden, grayling and lake trout are plentiful throughout the summer, but most abundant in June, and again in late August, September and October. Northern pike are available year-round."

Of the Iliamna tributaries, the Newhalen River is one of the more popular for salmon, grayling, rainbow and char. When gusty winds keep anglers on the ground, like it did to us the next day, the Newhalen beckons.

Several boats from Iliamna village lined the banks of the Newhalen, their dew-flecked engine cowlings shimmering in the morning sun. On a nearby hill, cut alder pole racks sagged under the weight of dried sockeye salmon. The intermingling of the old ways with the new is the way of life in many Alaska bush villages. But there wasn't anything old about the way the first rainbow hammered a lure we were drifting. The fish, a sleek five-pounder, erupted out of the river with gills shaking and tail thrashing.

"It's a small one," Will said. "The big eight-pounders rarely jump. Instead, they hug bottom and thrash around."

Since I was primarily a shoreline wader, Will's method—albeit simple—took some getting used to. We would motor up to the rapids, cut the engine and drift down the side currents over water four to six-feet deep. Along the breaklines, sockeye salmon were in various stages of spawning. Char, grayling and rainbow surrounded the sockeye redds, and were not the least bit hesitant about chasing down whatever we longlined behind the boat. It didn't matter what we used; flies, spoons and drift lures were equally as effective. We all caught rainbows that ranged from two to seven pounds.

Later that afternoon, Adela and I walked up the Newhalen to try fly fishing. Will made casts to deep-holding grayling in a backeddy, while Adela and I waded the shoreline below the rapids and roll cast for char and rainbows hugging near the river's gravel breakline. Casting flies in strong wind into the backeddies for char and rainbow was work, but nevertheless a relaxing sort of fun.

The gusts from the encroaching storm whipped the river's greenish surface to a white-capped foam. The shoreline alders lashed each other like buggy whips. On the opposite shoreline, a pair of youngsters armed with a .22 pistol began taking potshots at spawning sockeye salmon. I yelled at them, but they couldn't hear me in the gusting wind.

I lost my desire to fish, and sat on the bank and began chipping the ice out of my guides. Adela had a strike, but lost the fish on the first jump. Memories of other Iliamna waters such as Gibralter, Lower Talarik, the Copper, and Alagnak came to mind, where in years past I had tussled with husky rainbow trout ranging from three to 12 pounds. I had my moments of glory on Iliamna, moments where I could have hung up my rods for the rest of my life and be content. Now I was experiencing one of the horrors.

The shots continued, and I mentally jerked with each report, as if the shots were striking me. Then the kids stopped and walked on. In respect for the fish that I'm sure died, I did not fish the remainder of the day.

Standing on a lichen-encrusted rock, the howling wind purged my distraught. It was as if the lake spoke directly to me through the ears of my soul. She held no animosity toward these boys, and the salmon would continue to return, despite the abuse shown that day. If the lake could forgive, could I do anything less?

Later that evening, Will and I tied up some "guaranteed" flies for the grayling and lake trout we would pursue the next day. George asked if we wanted to fish already known hotspots, or to explore a few seldom-fished waters. We chose to explore the Lake Clark region, located north of Iliamna.

Flying to Lake Clark was a memorable experience. Bull moose sparred in the forests below, and herds of caribou migrated atop long, snake-like eskers left from the last Great Ice Age. Although many are greatly diminished in size, alpine glaciers still hang from mountaintops in Lake Clark Pass. If the weather is cooperating, you

Guided fly-out trips usually offer elaborate lunches complete with a variety of appetizers and refreshments. When requested, fresh salmon is grilled, and basted with a lemon butter/herb sauce. Seldom are there leftovers.

won't regret taking a flightseeing tour through the pass. I've flown through it countless times, and each time I do, goosebumps rise on my arm. The ice-gouged mountainsides, rocky spires, long, feathery waterfalls, and lush river bottomlands offer as much if not more excitement than a day of fishing.

George flew over Lake Clark, pumped down the flaps on the Beaver and landed near a gushing outlet stream that emptied into the emerald-hued lake.

While our guide, Randy, prepared a gravel bar for our four-course lunch, we rigged up. We cast upstream, and the current whisked our flies into the lake. The flies never made it past the first boil, which signaled a drop-off. A large, sail-finned grayling hit Adela's stonefly with a punch worthy of a fish twice its size. Another grayling of equal size nailed my offering with a bit less gusto. Both fish raised their dorsals in the current, creating twice the drag and three times the fun. Once in hand, they were cold and crisp to the touch, and emitted a soft, thyme-like fragrance. It reminded me of the grayling's Latin name Thymallus, which refers to this unique trait.

While Adela, George, and Randy started to make inroads into the cut salami, cheese and various spread appetizers, I switched to a half-ounce Crippled Herring and a light-action rod and level wind reel. After a power cast, I tight-lined the lure to bottom. Twenty-feet down, I felt a familiar jar and reared back. The line pulsed with the power of a gyrating lake trout. I fought that laker for 10 minutes before bringing it to hand. As I loosened the single hook from its upper kype, I learned this fish was far from defeated. With seeming devilment in its eye, it turned and sunk its needle-like teeth into my thumb. Surprise, more than pain, caused me to laugh.

"Guess I deserve it for sticking this piece of wire into your jaw," I said as I pried the trout's mouth open with my free hand and removed my bleeding thumb. I gently placed the fish back in the water. With a flick of its tail, it slowly eased down the greenish-hued drop-off. Eighteen lake trout later, I gave in to the pangs of hunger and watched Adela partake in catching both lakers and grayling on her ultralight spinning rod.

Flying back to Iliamna at 1,700 feet, we discussed other adventures in the Iliamna region, the Mulchatna kings in July, the trophy pike in the numerous tundra lakes and of course, the dime-bright rainbow trout of the Kvichak. I had fished them all, and thoughts of various trips caused my mind to wander to an Iliamna trout I hooked earlier that week.

The husky five-pounder had a vibrant greenish-blue dorsal with just a hint of pink on its chunky flanks. Like a bellows, the gills fanned the flame of life deep inside the fish. I kept the camera stashed, and simply enjoyed studying the fish. While appreciating the exquisite make-up of each scale's guanine crystals, I philosophized.

It's not hard to take Alaska sportfish for granted, especially in an environment where catching 50 or more fish per day is common. But Iliamna sportfish are experts at pulling heartstrings. These are fish whose ancestors have remained wild and untouched through thousands of years of evolution. But that was before man appeared on the scene. Perhaps eventually, stocked fish will intermingle with these survivors and weaken their strain. Maybe pollution will decimate their numbers. I sincerely hope not. In the interim, let's appreciate the opportunity to catch and release Iliamna sportfish. Despite the problems with subsistence, overfishing, crowds and litter—problems that many watersheds in Alaska also share—the Iliamna area is still a remarkable, awe-inspiring fishery. Try it this year and see for yourself.

Planning Your Trip

WHEN TO GO

First choose what species you want to pursue, then choose a time to fish the Iliamna area. Rainbow trout fishing is best in early June and again in October. Resident species such as grayling, pike, char and lake trout are available summer long. Salmon are available from June through October.

WHAT TO TAKE

Because the waters surrounding Iliamna offer such a variety of fishing opportunities and situations, carry a selection of rods and equipment suited for all of Alaska's sportfish and conditions. It includes: an ultralight spinning outfit with four-pound mono, and a medium-action spinning or level-wind rig for salmon, pike and char. If fishing the big rivers, like the Mulchatna, for kings, pack a 7 foot, medium-heavy rod and a level-wind Ambassadeur or similar reel filled with 20-pound mono.

Fly fishing gear should include a 3 to 4-weight rod for grayling and Dollies, a 6 to 7-weight for medium-sized rainbow, char and smaller salmon, and a 10-weight for kings, pike and casting large streamers on windy days. Salmon reels should be anti-reverse, filled with 200 yards or more of 30-pound backing. You'll need a full complement of sink-tip lines, with extra spools filled with floating and full-sink lines. Quality reels with solid drags are also imperative for char and trout.

Flies should cover all fishing conditions. They include Glo-Bug imitations, two-egg marabous, nondescript nymphs, black bivisibles, woolly worms, Salcha pinks, Sherry's deliverers, coronations, blue smolts, Baker busters, Alaska Perry flies, and bulky, gaudy flies preferably tied with fluorescent materials for murky water conditions. Lures include one-ounce Gibbs Krocs in silver and metallic blue, chartreuse and rainbo prism tape; Pro-Guide spinners in fluorescent red; Gibbs Kit-i-Mat spoons and Dardevles in fluorescent red and chartreuse, Storm Magnum Wee Warts in gold and fluorescent pink; and topwater plugs for pike that include Poe's Ace-In-The-Hole and Heddon Torpedoes in frog and silver/metallic blue. Drift lures such as Spin-N-Glos in all sizes take a variety of fish under all conditions. Take plenty of ball-bearing swivels, various drifting weights, sunscreen, polarized sunglasses and insect repellent. I recommend neoprene waders for all-day fishing, and hip boots for exploring streams and walking cross-country to various fishing locales. Pack tackle in small boxes to be carried in a vest or small daypack. All rods should be collapsible, and carried in small rod tubes. Avoid large cases, as they are difficult to fit into small planes.

HOW TO GET THERE

From Anchorage, fly a commercial airline to Iliamna or King Salmon.

Do-it-yourselfers can charter out of Soldotna, Kenai, Homer or King Salmon.

WHERE TO STAY
There is no shortage of lodges and fish camps in the Iliamna region. Do-it-yourselfers should consider camping a good distance away from major thoroughfares, such as the mouth of inlet streams, where daily lodge traffic concentrates. Another possibility is floating one or more of the major rivers such as the Kvichak, Koktuli or Alagnak.

APPROXIMATE COSTS
Depending on services provided, expect to pay anywhere from $800 to $4,000 per week for bare-bones outfitted to full-service lodge accommodations in this region. Do-it-yourself fly-outs run anywhere from $400 to $1,200 or more.

WHO TO CONTACT
For a listing of guides, outfitters and do-it-yourself services, turn to page 208, "Free Information To Plan Your Trip."

10 Adventure

Autumn on northern Alaska's Kobuk River not only offers outstanding sheefish opportunities, but also spectacular fall colors and few insects.

Make A Date with a Shee

EACH YEAR IN LATE AUGUST, I faithfully make a pilgrimage to fish the Kobuk River, located in the southern shadow of the glacially-carved Brooks Range of northern Alaska.

The two-hour bush-plane flight from Fairbanks is long, but offers time for reflection. Indeed, there is much to reflect upon. One topic is my sanity. Why do I spend hundreds of dollars on chartering a flight to fish the Kobuk when I have good salmon and grayling fishing a few miles from my home?

The answer is simple. All of Alaska's trout and salmon rivers are special to me, but only a few offer qualities that excite my spirit, causing me to laugh like a schoolboy at play. The Kobuk is such a river.

From my airplane seat I look down and see the Kobuk, appearing as forlorn as a freshly cut rose tossed into a dirt field. The river's currents are modest, and in many sections, its complexion is the color of strong tea. These are just two reasons why many anglers ignore this river. Instead, they search for dime-bright salmon and trout in clear, coastal waters, replete with their luxurious lodges and armada of riverboats.

I'm thankful for the illusion. For those who know the Kobuk,

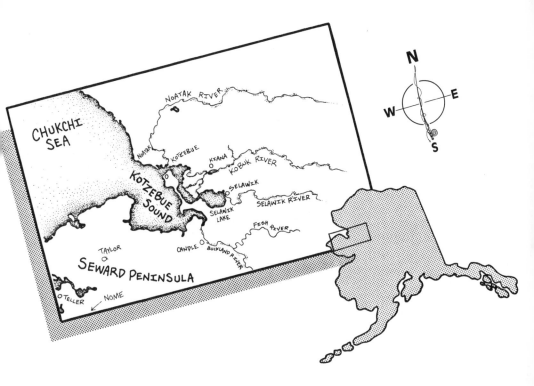

this comely appearance is a mask that hides one of the most unique fisheries in North America.

As the floatplane disappears over the distant mountains, I slowly view this river bottomland with the somber reverence accorded a truly great fishery. Intricate mosaics of dried algae and crisp yellow birch leaves decorate the sun-bleached gravel bars. To the right, the low rhythmic notes of water lapping the shoreline harmonize with the racing melody of a feeder creek. Side sloughs are strewn with beaver cuttings, and the tangy-sweet fragrance of castoreum spices the air. On distant sandbars, geese give their farewell honks as they prepare to fly south over the rocky spires of the Brooks Range.

The swan song of summer is in its final verse, and soon the river will sleep under a covering of ice and snow. Yet, if you listen carefully, you can hear the riffles sing a melody of life and excitement.

It starts with a tail slap, and builds to a crescendo of heavy splashes that ring the cool steel of twilight. Look closely, squinting through the glow that's the remnant of the midnight sun and you'll see inconnu; large, heavy-bodied fish with scales the size and sheen of newly minted quarters. Look closer and you'll notice they have a dark lateral line and underslung jaw which greatly resemble those of a snook. Twenty pounders are common; the 30 to 50-pound fish are the heavyweight spawners, reckless in their spawning ritual.

Sheefish are also called "tarpon of the north" because of their acrobatic displays once hooked. To hook shee consistently, anglers must have fishing savvy as well as properly honed presentation skills.

Put down your fishing rod, listen, and allow yourself to become a part of the inconnu experience. Permit me the honor of introducing you.

The early French-Canadian explorers gave the fish its most common name, "poisson inconnu" meaning "unknown fish." Biologists theorize that the inconnu probably originated in Siberia and migrated to arctic and sub-arctic Alaska during or after the Bering Land Bridge era. The fish slowly evolved into an esturine-anadromous species, meaning it spends its winters in the brackish waters of deltas, inlets and tidal lakes in northern coastal Alaska, Canada and Siberia.

Aesthetics aside, the first night's camp near an inconnu spawning grounds is the wilderness equivalent to staying in a thin-walled hotel with squeaky beds.

Unlike salmon and other species that dig redds in deep pools, the inconnu, or more commonly known as sheefish, spawn in shallows during hours of darkness. In a series of splashes and wake-producing runs directly beneath the surface, the females extrude their eggs and the males fertilize them. This spawning ritual is seldom viewed by visiting anglers. Once seen, however, it is remembered and appreciated for a lifetime. It is what draws both anglers and fish to this remote northcountry wilderness.

However, there is one difference. After an hour or two, the infrequent sounds of spawning sheefish can lull you to sleep. But you'll be kept awake by arctic grayling, the hooligans of the side currents. For hours they'll splash frantically through the gravel riffles, gorging on free-floating sheefish eggs. Of course, the very thought of catching sheefish, also known as "tarpon of the north," can also keep you wide-eyed with excitement all night long. When you can't take it any more, unpack your tackle and limber up your fishing rods. It's time to go fishing.

Before making that first cast, a word of caution. Sheefish are conquerors. If your allegiance is to salmon or trout, battle a sheefish and you'll question your fidelity. For instance, the strike of a sheefish is classic. Don't expect the dainty slurp of a grayling or trout taking a dry fly, or the grab-and-run tendencies of Kenai king salmon. No. Sheefish mean business. When they inhale a fly or lure, and I do mean inhale, it's a jolt that shocks, as well as amazes. If you're quick enough to retaliate with a solid hookset, and lucky enough to bury the barb into one of the two, inch-square areas of soft mouth tissue (the rest is nearly impenetrable bone) hold on for a series of out-of-water, head-shaking acrobatics that would do a saltwater tarpon proud.

The sheefish has skyrocketed in popularity during its short history in sportfishing circles. Only since the early 1970s, when air access opened up prime sheefish grounds in Alaska, and biologists became more familiar with this only predatory member of the whitefish family, have sheefish received the recognition they deserve as a sportfish species.

Of Alaska's nine major stocks of sheefish, those in the Yukon River tributaries of the Nowitna, Minto Flats (Tanana River), Porcupine, Salmon Fork of the Black, and upper Yukon rivers are non-anadromous stocks. Those of the Kuskokwim, Lower Yukon, Koyuk and Kobuk-Selawik rivers are esturine-anadromous species. This means sheefish spend winters in the brackish waters of inlets, tidal lakes and deltas of Alaska's Bering Sea. There they feed heavily on smelt and other forage fish species. In late June, they head upstream on their spawning migration. And after spawning in late September and early October, it's a race downstream to the wintering grounds in an effort to beat ice-up.

The largest sheefish in North America hail from the Kobuk-Selawik drainage. There, anglers find sizable runs of shee that can reach weights of up to 60 pounds. While I've never caught a 60-pounder, I have caught plenty of shee in the 30 to 45-pound category.

Nick Jennings is likewise familiar with the allure of the Kobuk sheefish. For over eight years he has guided anglers to prime sheefish waters from his remote camp in the heart of the Brooks Range, near the headwaters of the mighty Kobuk.

Jennings takes pride in introducing anglers to sheefish. During his exhibits at sport shows in the Lower 48, he says the sheefish mount in his booth receives the most inquiries.

"People are impressed by the size of the fish and its shape," he said. "Another fact that impresses them is how old sheefish can get. A 10-pound fish may be as old as 10 years, while a 60-pounder may be 21 years or older. After I tell them about the spectacular fighting qualities of the species, they are ready to book a trip."

It wasn't always easy to interest anglers in sheefish. When I started to pursue sheefish in the mid-1970s, it was hard to interest major magazine editors in running a story on this species. "Too obscure to interest many of our readers," they said. Stories were nevertheless published in smaller publications by myself, sheefish biologist Ken Alt and a handful of other writers. The fish's popularity grew. Several years ago, the International Game Fish Association—caretakers of both fresh and saltwater sportfishing records—helped to popularize the species even more by opening up a sheefish category to line-class records.

Since, Jennings said several anglers have succeeded in setting a handful of records. He related how these record catches were set while we flew in his plane to the Kobuk.

"All the records were vacant in the beginning," he said. "Now, they're all filled. However, anglers can still catch a line-class record sheefish if they know what to do and where to go."

A review of the IGFA's World Record Game Fishes confirms that most record fish listed on line categories ranging from 2 to 50-pound test weigh from 32 to 53 pounds. Jennings says these records can easily be beat. On another interesting note, all the entries have come from the Kobuk River or its drainages. Most record-book fish have been caught in August and early September.

"August is the best month for sheefish," Jennings said over the drone of his Cessna 206. "Other than large grayling, lake trout and arctic char, sheefish are what people are interested in catching this time of year.

"The best action usually occurs after first light, and lasts until noon. Sheefish tend to hold up during mid day, usually in deep holes or in and around backwater sloughs. Action picks up again around 5 p.m. During the peak of the run, however, action is continuous all day long."

As we flew over the Kobuk and searched for prime sheefish spots and possibly a sheefish holding in a shallow side current, Jennings offered some advice on where-to-fish. I always had best success in the main river current, but Jenning's approach was different.

"I prefer to locate and fish the sloughs near heavy currents," he said. "The fish will concentrate in the quiet water to take a breather before heading back out again. You can also fish the current for fish that are passing through. Such a location offers the best of both fishing situations."

Once you find a good sheefish hole, set up camp and fish it for several days. Since sheefish migrations peak at various times of the day, for best success vary your fishing times.

With that, Jennings lowered the flaps and circled over a wide-mouthed slough that emptied its muskeg-stained water into the Kobuk. In the light olive-green shallows, I spotted three sheefish. To the right of the slough mouth, grayling dimpled the surface. We landed downriver and taxied back to the slough.

While unloading our gear, Jennings expressed his optimism about the fishing possibilities.

"You should do really well," he said. "The fish are here, and there are chum salmon near that far shore." He climbed into the plane. "I'll return to pick you up in two days."

While searching for a campsite, my wife and fishing partner Adela and I discovered that we were not the first ones to use this area. The bank was a well-traveled secondary road system for bears and moose. Not wanting to get trampled in the middle of the night, we pitched our tent in the protective confines of the alders.

We expected to do well, but not on the fifth cast. A silver and blue attractor pattern was inhaled seconds before my line bellied out downstream. Although it had been a year since I last felt the hard "thud" of a sheefish strike, there was no mistaking it.

I reared back on the rod. The fish was a bulldogger. Trying to pull him off the bottom was like attempting to pull the plug from the river. When the fish finally relented to my pressure, he showed his displeasure by taking to the air in a cataclysm of spray and body twists. Not once, but four times. It was the type of action that keeps an angler smiling long into the night.

The fish fought for another few minutes before succumbing to the pressure of rod and line. The fish's performance was impressive; more so once I caught sight of it, a small yet sleek 16-pounder. To my dismay the fish had engulfed the fly, and was hooked on the edge of a gill raker, three inches from the edge of its bone-rimmed

Fly fishing for sheefish is a consummate challenge, as the largest fish stick to deep holes in slow-moving backwater sloughs. The larger and flashier the fly, the better. Here, Chris Batin unhooks a 15-pounder that was hooked too deeply to be released.

mouth. It took a few moments to realize the fish would not make it. With great remorse and sorrow, I dispatched the fish.

Looking on the brighter side of things, we soon had in our makeshift grass cooler some of the finest gourmet-eating fish available in the northcountry. Grayling are excellent table fish, but when it comes to filling a hungry stomach, a sheefish is superb. Its white, flaky meat is delicately flavored, with a non-fishy, pleasant aroma similar to that of fresh herbs.

That evening, we added a slice of butter and dash of tarragon and white pepper, and baked the fish in the coals of an open campfire. We've yet to find better eating elsewhere.

Jennings had been right about morning being the best time for sheefish action. Adela hooked and lost a fish, while I had several good strikes before I was finally able to get a good hookset. I knew from the slow headshake and thrashing that the fish was a good one. After 15 minutes of battle, I eased a 45-pounder to shore. After posing for a few photos, the sheefish snapped his tail a few times and disappeared into the Kobuk.

Towards noon, we explored the fishing in other areas of the river that included riffles, pools, and cut banks. We didn't catch a sheefish the entire afternoon. However, around 6 p.m. the action started to pick up. Using a fly rod, we caught and released numerous sheefish in the 15 to 20-pound range. And best of all, we had yet to see another angler or plane flying overhead.

After 9 p.m. on the Kobuk, priorities change among the river's inhabitants. The sheefish start thinking about spawning, and the ruling scepter is given to the countless numbers of arctic grayling that begin feeding with wild abandon. Unlimbering lighter fly rods, we decided to have some fun.

Floating the Kobuk River in mid to late August is a popular way to explore sheefish country. Anglers can also expect to catch northern pike, grayling and dog salmon as well as an occasional char.

The number of grayling thriving in the Kobuk is incredulous. If I may exaggerate only slightly, they are about as numerous as the water molecules in the river itself. Adela and I walked out to a riffle about 15 feet from our tent, and let our fly lines dangle as we started a debate over the right pattern to use. The fish made the decision for us. Almost immediately, numerous six to eight-inch grayling leaped for our Number 12 black gnats. On numerous occasions, several would jump out at once, colliding in mid air. If the runts of the species were so active, what about the larger ones? We would soon find out.

I cast a size 10 blue dun. Nothing but small fish. Then a black gnat. More small fish. Enough was enough. While Adela amused herself with the fish-a-cast activity near shore, I waded out to a gravel bar and tied on a weighted stonefly nymph. Typically, large grayling don't move as fast as their smaller, more mobile offspring. Therefore, it's imperative to find the large fish, and get the fly down to them as quickly as possible.

The strategy worked. The line twitched as the fly was sinking. An 18-incher with a sweeping dorsal fin knifed upstream, then down, before relenting to the steady pressure of the fly rod. Twenty-five casts and 25 fish later, I walked back to shore. It was impossible to get a proper drift without a grayling inhaling the nymph. And these were large fish, from 14 to 18 inches. It's the type of problem you don't mind having.

I handed my rod to Adela, who began to giggle and squeal her way through a series of much larger fish. I called it a day. Part of the sheefish experience is savoring the moment. I stretched out on the sandy gravel bank, with a small campfire going and fish rising all around, and thanked the Lord for moments like this. They help make life complete.

113

Mark Ketscher examines an Eskimo grave house on a bluff overlooking the Pah River. Such gravesites are commonly seen throughout interior and western Alaska.

The next morning, we were making good catches of sheefish when Jennings flew in to pick us up. The largest sheefish that morning had been a 28-pounder, which we released unharmed.

It was tough to pack up camp. The tart aroma of ripe cranberries had permeated our tent and sleeping bags. Grayling milled around in the nearest pool, anxiously awaiting to attack any natural or imitation insect that happened to fly or drift by. And out in the main river were sheefish, perhaps a dozen, perhaps 50 or more. I wanted to catch and hug each one, but instead I settled for giving them a simple nod of respect and appreciation.

We took our time disassembling our rods. This was wilderness fishing at its finest, where life is laid back, the fishing spectacular, and northcountry autumn hangs heavy in the air. But I knew we would revisit the Kobuk another time, for other experiences, other adventures. And of course, we'll be back for the wonderful inconnu. After all, shee's a mighty fine catch.

Author's Note: While this book was in production, Nick Jennings died in an automobile accident on Alaska's Richardson Highway. Jennings loved the Brooks Range greatly, which was evident by the enthusiasm in his voice whenever he talked about sheefish, the mountains or its wildlife. He'll be greatly missed by friends and anglers alike.

Tips for Catching Sheefish

Sheefish can be hooked on most any type of sport tackle. Here are guidelines to follow for maximizing your fish-in-hand successes:

First, you'll need a medium-action or stiff-spined rod with plenty of backbone. Sheefish have bone-hard mouths that repel the strongest, most sharpest of hooks and hooksets. I prefer to use a 7 1/2-foot rod and a level-wind Ambassadeur reel with 12 to 17-pound test monofilament in clear or green. Fluorescent lines spook fish. Spinning rods work as well, as do fly rods. Sheefish I have hooked with my 10-weight graphite fly rod gave it a thorough workout. Anything less than a 10-weight and you'll be under-equipped. The heftier rod also allows you to cast the large, gaudy flies that sheefish prefer.

Use streamer and attractor fly patterns with plenty of flash. Herring patterns on 2 and 1/0 hooks are not too large for sheefish. Also, flies tied with Flashabou work well, as do Alaska Perry flies, Alaskabou patterns and Las Vegas Showgirl patterns in silver and blue tinsel.

Sheefish congregate in side sloughs and their adjacent deep-water areas. Here, a weighted fly comes in handy. It's best to add the weight during construction of the fly, rather than add it on at streamside. Always have a few unweighted flies for that occasional shallow-water fish.

In sloughs and pools, find sheefish at depths anywhere from three to 12 or more feet deep. Overall, expect five feet. A 400 to 800-grain line works best in the heavy main current, while a 10-foot sink-tip is good for side sloughs and longer casts.

With flies, slow motion is the key. Strip the fly a few inches, then allow it to drop. Vary the retrieve, working up to as much as two-foot strips. Various flies, lines and currents will behave differently. It's important to experiment until you find a combination that works.

Remember that the flash principle also applies with spinning and casting lures. It's important to use lures that exhibit the right type of flash. After 16 years of fishing for sheefish, I still consider spoons to be the No. 1 spinning lure. But not any spoon will work. Here's a tip: Before purchasing a spoon, hold it in subdued light. Turn the lure in the light, and watch for the intensity of the flash. If blackish, the spoon is chrome plated and won't catch as many sheefish as will a silver-plated spoon, which has a sharp, silver flash to it. My experience has shown that the latter is more visible to the sheefish, and triggers more strikes.

For the main river currents pack plenty of one-ounce spoons in both long and normal configurations. For the slower side currents, 1/2 or 3/4-ounce spoons do the job nicely. For instance, avoid spoons that roll and twist in the current. Spoons such as the Gibbs Koho and Swedish Pimple have the proper action.

Fishing technique is simple. Cast upstream, and immediately reel or strip in any slack. Wait until you feel the "tap-tap" of bottom, and slowly begin your retrieve. It's imperative that you keep the lure within inches of the bottom, where sheefish are found. Once the lure bellies out in the current, reel in and repeat.

Always use single hooks. Trebles do far too much damage, as the sheefish typically inhales the lure with enough force to lodge it in the back of its throat. Treble hooks will bury into the gill rakers or gills, causing the fish to hemorrhage to death. A single hook will usually miss this critical area, and hook the fish in the small, soft portion of the mouth.

If you don't have a strike after 10 to 15 minutes of fishing, change lures or flies. Depending on weather and light conditions, sheefish can be finicky toward lures.

While camping out or float fishing the Kobuk, be sure to boil all water before drinking, to prevent giardiasis. There is plenty of bird, beaver and mammal activity in the area. Also, drop-off anglers should pack a small inflatable for crossing the side sloughs. The craft will help in expanding your fishing area.

If you kill a sheefish, keep it as cold as possible. If allowed to get too warm, or left to sit for hours on the bank or in the river, the flesh loses its delectable flavor.

And last but not least, limit your take of sheefish. They are an extremely slow-growing fish, and should be enjoyed sparingly, lest they suffer the same fate as other wild stocks have faced here in Alaska and in the Lower 48.

Planning Your Trip

WHEN TO GO
The best sheefishing on the Kobuk takes place in early to mid August, with the run slowly tapering off toward the latter part of the month.

WHAT TO TAKE
Local lodges offer all of the tackle and gear you'll need. A do-it-yourself trip, however, requires you to be totally self-sufficient. Shipping gear to the Kobuk can be expensive, costing 50 cents or more per pound. If possible, keep gear to within 60 pounds per person, excluding inflatable boat.

HOW TO GET THERE
Fly to Fairbanks, and reserve a seat on a commercial flight from Fairbanks to Bettles. From there charter with an air taxi operator to the Kobuk River. Cost is roughly $800 per aircraft. Also consider chartering a flight from Fairbanks. Cost is roughly $1200 to $1600 round trip, depending on type of aircraft and location of drop camp.

WHERE TO STAY
While this is primarily a do-it-yourself trip, a handful of lodges do offer accommodations. Overnight accommodations are also available in Bettles.

WHO TO CONTACT
For a listing of guides, outfitters and do-it-yourself services, turn to page 208, "Free Information to Plan Your Trip."

11 Adventure

This arctic char fell for a quickly stripped fly worked through a side current on the Little Togiak River. The fish was released unharmed.

World-Class Fishing Indulgence at Bristol Bay

I HAVE A CONFESSION TO MAKE.

As editorial director of Alaska Angler Publications, my winter months are filled with hectic schedules and fast-paced business meetings. Sometimes they are too stress-filled, and something snaps.

My first breakdown took place in late June. I was neck deep in seven different deadlines when the stress of the office environment finally took its toll. Co-workers began to show concern over the abrupt change in my behavior. Indeed, there was plenty to be concerned about. I daydreamed and doodled at business meetings, window shopped for hip boots instead of Gucci loafers, and spent long hours reading *The Alaska Angler*® instead of *The Wall Street Journal*.

To me, the malady was obvious. Alaska's Bristol Bay region was calling my name. Within two days I traded our four-story office complex for the clear waters of the bay's Togiak River. I would fish, and find inner peace and solitude in Nature.

The inner peace and solitude were short-lived.

As I stripped the fly through the clear, shallow waters of the Togiak, my upper torso tensed with anxiety and my eyes widened at

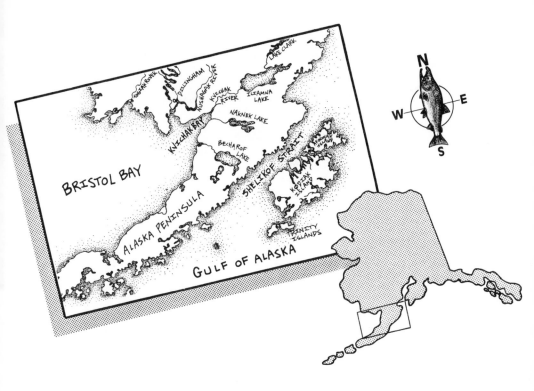

the sight before me. A torpedo-shaped, 48-pound king salmon appeared beneath the swirling currents. Both fish and fly were on an intercept course.

I stripped the fly in faster to irritate the fish. Seeing the fly was escaping, the territorial salmon flared its tail and shot forward to grab the fly. The black-rimmed jaws opened and came down with seething aggression, chewing the chenille body to shreds.

A burst of adrenalin triggered my hookset, which ignited the salmon into explosive fury. Like a blade of grass in a windstorm, my heavyweight fly rod dipped and darted in a blur of undulations. I dug my heels into the gravel and leaned back heavily on the rod.

The salmon sizzled upriver for 50 yards before cutting a hard right, where it partially beached itself on a sandbar. Before I could run over and subdue the fish, the 12-inch-wide tail thrashed the shallows like a high-speed mixer. Sand and water shot into the air, and within seconds, the salmon was back in its element.

Without hesitation, the fish kicked in its afterburners. It erupted in a cataclysm of spray once, twice, three times, screeched through a couple of 70-degree turns and bounced off a gravel bar. My rod bucked spasmodically, and the flyline backing hummed with tension.

Twenty minutes seemed like 20 years as the fish gyrated, sulked and thrashed its river confines. Even though my face was frozen in

Ron Kahlenbeck with a king salmon he caught while fishing the Nushagak River. Many lodges in the western Bristol Bay region fish the major king run on the "Nush" in mid to late June. Angler success is often high.

Opposite page: Pilot Leonard Cory fishing in the Wind River area of the upper Wood-Tikchik chain. Rainbow, char and grayling are abundant, and the scenery is spectacular.

an ear-to-ear grin, my arms and back ached from tension. And I wasn't alone in my fatigue. My leader was badly nicked and frayed. The prognosis was not good. I had to act now, or lose the battle.

Butterflies flew haphazardly in my stomach and chest as I muscled the fish onto its side. The salmon's head dwarfed my outstretched hand. Its gills pumped water rhythmically, like a bellows injecting new life into its indefatigable spirit. The upturned eye was wild and alive with power. The subsequent staredown was intimidating. It was as if the salmon dared me to touch it.

I reached out, clamped my pliers onto the barbless hook, and with a flick of the wrist released my prize. After holding motionless for a few seconds, the king slowly eased into the current. Never acknowledging defeat, the fish maintained its dignity as it disappeared from sight. I nodded my head, and mentally saluted a gallant fighter.

Then it hit me with the force of a spiked volleyball. The euphoric high short-circuited my stamina. My hands trembled and racing heartbeat pounded in my head. Those butterflies had metamorphosed into the huge, gastro-intestinal type and were about to carry me away. What I really needed was a belt of Yukon Jack to quench the fire of excitement that singed my nerve endings.

But it was too late. Out in the current I saw another big king porpoise. Pulling myself together, I retied leader and fly for the next round. I had six more days of fishing ahead of me, and had heard stories of catching 10 to 20 kings per day from this very

watershed. Realizing I would possibly fish myself into oblivion, a bit of fishing insanity took hold. I knelt down and kissed a huge boulder. "Alaska, you're the greatest!" I said.

Fifteen minutes later, I was laughingly chasing down another king.

Indeed, the Bristol Bay region of southwest Alaska is the empress of the sportfishing realm. Reigning above the 58th parallel, she is gracefully veiled in sapphire-blue ocean waters, winding wilderness rivers, and mirror-like mountain lakes. Although regal in appearance, Bristol Bay is a seductive mistress, tempting you to experience the pinnacle of the world's best sportfishing—complete with its many passions. She'll entice you royally with king salmon and princely arctic char, stately arctic grayling and knightly silver salmon. With her you'll experience a fishing that you never knew existed, an excitement that you've never felt before. And after sampling her fishing wares, Bristol Bay will sedate you with her sensual beauty; the blush of midnight sun on the cheeks of her alpine face, or the mysterious, emerald-green gaze of her coastal forests. Indeed, most anglers cannot resist her charm and easily fall into temptation. Once they do, they're hooked.

To fish Bristol Bay is to know the standard by which the world's best sportfishing is judged. And there are about 75 lodges in the bay area that would like to introduce you to this standard. But to offer the ultimate Alaska fishing adventure, lodges must provide more than just world-class fishing. They must cater to your every whim. At some of the finest you can dine on king crab and New York steak, sample the best California wines, or sip Bailey's and coffee while relaxing fish-tired muscles in a bubbling jacuzzi. Of the hundreds of anglers who enjoy the ultimate Alaska fishing experience each year, many choose Wood River Lodge, located in the Wood River-Tikchik Lake area of Bristol Bay.

The lodge is an island oasis in a sea of wilderness fishing indulgence. Forget about roughing it in a tent or trapper's cabin. Upon arriving at the lodge, relax in a private, cedar cabin with carpeted rooms and indoor bath. In the evening, the bed covers will be turned back, the heat turned up a bit to take off the chill, and European chocolates placed on your pillow.

Why this pampering? You'll need all your energy to tackle the sportfish of Bristol Bay. The staff at Wood River Lodge realizes this, and makes life for their guests as simple and pleasurable as possible.

Morning arrives quickly the first full day at Wood River Lodge. I speak from experience. On a July morning, at 6:30 a.m., cohostess Vonnie Ortman lightly knocked on our cabin door, entered, and placed a pot of hot coffee on our nightstand. My roommate and uncle, Bob Batin and I had our first cup of coffee in bed. Oh yes. The man outside the door carrying a shotgun is manager Don McCarley. He's Vonnie's bodyguard. But we weren't the threat Don was concerned about.

"In early morning and late evening, there will be one or more brown bears strolling through camp," he said. "That brings up Lodge Rule 1. People knock and announce their presence. Brown bears scratch and go 'Wooof.'"

Sound wisdom.

Deciding what to fish for in the Bristol Bay area is as difficult a decision as where to fish. The decisions are made at breakfast, an elaborate affair consisting of eggs benedict, hash browns, oatmeal, gourmet pancakes and the standard assortment of fruit, bacon, sausage and lots of hot coffee and fruit juice.

At the breakfast table, Don briefed the 12 guests on lodge procedure. The clients who faced the large picture window were mesmerized by the rainbow and char dimpling the surface of the Agulowak River, less than 100 feet away.

"This week, there are 10 out of 11 species of sportfish available to you," he said. "These are arctic grayling, northern pike, arctic char, Dolly Varden, rainbow trout, lake trout, and king, chum, pink and sockeye salmon. What do you want to fish for?"

Like kids in a candy store, Bob and I wanted to sample all at once. After much discussion, we chose a wilderness fly-out for northern pike.

Of the 54,700 square-mile area of Bristol Bay and the

Kuskokwim, the lodge conducts most of its fishing in the massive Wood River-Tikchik Lakes area and the Togiak National Wildlife Refuge. Because there are no roads dissecting these wilderness areas, the lodge flies guests to most of the fishing spots in two Cessna 206 and one Cessna 185 floatplanes.

"These are more than just fly-outs, they are adventures," said lodge guest Guy Rodrigues of Alahambra, California. "There's a certain thrill about having a $100,000 airplane at your disposal."

Adventure is an understatement. Each plane holds three anglers, pilot and gear. Although there is excellent fishing in front of the lodge, chief pilot and lodge owner Ken Stockholm tries to preserve that for after-dinner fishing.

"After a nine-hour day of fishing, some anglers still can't get enough," he said as he taxied us onto Lake Nerka and readied the floatplane for take-off. "The Agulowak River, which runs in front of the lodge, offers plenty of salmon, trout, grayling and char. Sometimes we have anglers fishing until 2 a.m., and they rise again at 6 a.m. to fish before breakfast."

I glanced at Bob and turned red-faced. I was out until 1 a.m. the night before, casting for and catching rainbow trout. Some things a man just can't control.

Jovial and gray haired, Ken Stockholm is an experienced and respected pilot who is as much at home at the controls of a plane as he is in helping people catch fish. You'll need to press him, however, about his "extracurricular" activities during the winter and spring months. In addition to handling the logistics of booking and running the lodge, he is a professor of criminology at the University of Alaska-Fairbanks. His wife Helen, who serves as the

Angler Jim Oatfield discusses the merits of various patterns in his streamer collection with lodge owner Ken Stockholm.

lodge hostess, has a master's degree in criminology. She works for the University of Alaska Sea Grant program.

As the floatplane lifted off Lake Nerka, pathologist Dennis Wood, Bob and I studied the frontier ahead of us. My mind quickly turned to thinking about the only species of fish unavailable to us on this trip. It was the acrobatic silver salmon. Many years ago, Ken introduced several of us to this special strain of Bristol Bay salmon.

It was early September when he flew Paul and Sue Wagner and me to the lodge's outpost camp, located on a windswept gravel bar on the Nushagak River. In less than an hour, the three of us had forsaken Ken, our guide Troy Cowles, and for that matter, each other. We were lost in the pandemonium of trying to subdue spunky, tail-dancing 10 to 17-pound silvers.

Anglers often bet on the number of jumps a hooked silver will make. Our group was no different. Here's a tip I learned the hard way: You'll almost always lose if you bet less than five.

The three of us hooked no less than 40 fish that morning. Most were released, and one was fin-marked for shore lunch.

It was a meal to remember. Troy expertly filleted the husky salmon, and gently coated it with lemon-pepper and butter. He slow-steamed it in a cast-iron skillet over a driftwood fire, and fried up an accompaniment of seasoned potatoes and onions. To our surprise, he produced a selection of fresh vegetables and a bottle of white zinfandel. A pair of eagles flew overhead, and a porcupine later appeared on the far shore. During lunch, we watched a ribbon of silvers porpoise upriver.

"This is dining in the finest, most scenic restaurant in the world," Paul said. "The salmon fishing and wilderness wonder have given me a huge appetite. I bet there won't be any leftovers today." There wasn't.

Wood River Lodge, as seen from the middle of the Agulowak River, considered by many to be one of the finest rainbow trout waters in this region.

I snapped back to reality as Ken Stockholm circled Lake Nerka, and soon the plane's floats were cutting the glassy surface of the lake. We were fishing within 20 minutes. On the first cast, Dennis' fly landed on a reed. He tried to dislodge the fly by wiggling it, but a pike exploded from the water and grabbed it first. Dennis went wild.

The swans in the nearby marsh must have viewed the scene as a strange humanistic ritual. Three grown men were howling and sloshing through the water, chasing fish with black graphite fly rods. We enticed more than 80 pike into striking. At day's end, Dennis' fly was nothing more than a hook with a single strand of orange hair. Eventually, the pike chewed it down to the naked hook. And that's what we called it; the Naked Nothing. And it still caught fish.

The next morning our group met before breakfast and opted for a non-fly-out trip for arctic char on Lake Aleknagik. Char (which means elegant or beautiful), with its pinkish spots and golden flanks, sounds like a dainty, peaceful and relaxing species to pursue. We should have known better. After all, this was Bristol Bay.

Our guide, Duncan Oswald, anchored the boat at the lake inlet. The roily surface danced with the upsurging of river current of the Agulowak, deflected by large boulders far below the surface.

Oswald said the action would pick up any minute.

"Each summer, hundreds of char school up like mini-sharks at the mouths of the area rivers to gorge on the millions of out-migrating salmon smolt," he said.

Ten minutes passed. Twenty minutes passed. Bob had rigged up, but I was lazing around in the bow of the boat. Suddenly, the surface erupted in a series of boiling wakes. Salmon smolt jumped out of the water, trying to escape the feeding frenzy of hundreds of

When an unexpected downpour hits on a wilderness lake, an aircraft wing can serve as an adequate umbrella, allowing anglers to sit down, relax and enjoy lunch.

Opposite page: Paul Wagner is as pleased with his 30th silver salmon of the day as he was with his first. He was fishing southwest Alaska's Goodnews River in early September.

char below. Arctic terns folded their wings and crashed into the water head first. They emerged with two or three squiggly smolt, quickly swallowed them and again took to the air. As the feeding frenzy and avian whirlwind surrounded us, I frantically rigged up my fly and ultralight spinning rods.

From our seats we could see the massacre that was taking place beneath the boat. Indeed, hundreds of char darted all around, pushing the smolt to the surface. Using four-pound test line and an ultralight five-foot rod, Bob jigged his lure to imitate a fleeing smolt. Before it moved 10 feet, a husky five-pound char hammered it.

We crimped barbs. Changed lures. We fly fished. Fish were caught on all methods. We stopped counting at 50.

On the return up the Agulowak River late that afternoon, Duncan and I introduced Dennis to the sledgehammer strikes of river rainbows. In less than an hour, he had hooked a dozen fish. I felt complacent to sit back, observe and take a few photos. I had caught my share earlier that morning, while everyone else was in bed.

Once at the lodge, we noticed the guests, ourselves included, were moving around with a bit less zip in their walk. Obviously our actions indicated we were being too indulgent in our piscivorous pursuits. Yet we were enjoying every minute of it.

After a quick shower, we all met at the lodge for hors d'oeuvres of stuffed shrimp cocktail and shish kabob seasoned with a herb sauce. Ice from the self-serve bar tinkled amidst the flow of stories.

Dinner was an elaborate affair. Julie Catlett, a qualifier in Olympic cooking competition, prepared spectacular gourmet halibut, chicken and beef entries. The food flowed without end, and the trout kept rising on the Agulowak until mid-evening. When the food stopped, the fish stories took over.

"We caught over 60 fish today," said real estate appraiser John Chapman, who was fishing with his son, Owens.

"Owens kept getting all these strikes, but he wasn't hooking any fish and he started suffering from an inferiority complex," he said. "We learned that a fish had broken off his hook."

Alain De Weck and his wife, Christine, from Switzerland, celebrated his 60th birthday by taking the Wood River Luxury Cruise via the lodge's customized houseboat. Helen Stockholm served 15 different types of antipasto and cheeses while enroute to the first fishing spot on Lake Nerka. Co-hostess Sherry Cobb ensured that everyone's crystal champagne glass remained full. The skipper kept a watch out for wildlife. It wasn't long before everyone was taking photos of the cow and calf moose walking along the lakeshore.

Within an hour, the boat was at the first fishing hole. Guy Rodrigues made a few casts while the De Wecks relaxed on the deck in the 75-degree sunshine. Two hours later, the skipper called for a break. The tally was 42 arctic char from three to six pounds, and one sockeye salmon.

The break consisted of more finery. Helen served gourmet coffees and teas, smoked pheasant, chilled shrimp and crab, fresh strawberries, the famous Wood River Salmon Log, and a variety of dips, breads and crackers. Everyone agreed it was one of the finest gourmet lunches ever served on the lake.

"This is almost as good as my fly-out fishing trip yesterday for arctic grayling," Alain said. "I was the only one fishing this stream, and caught and released over 100 grayling on a fly."

By day six, we had caught nine of the 11 sportfish species. We didn't have time to pursue lake trout, and the silvers wouldn't be in for another two weeks. But we didn't care anymore. The 12 of us were sleeping in until breakfast, and spending the evenings watching the collection of videos of each other's trips. At Wood River, as well as a few other lodges, the guides videotape your entire day, and each guest receives a copy of their week's fishing highlights.

"A video is much better than photos," said guest Carl Tabet. "You can see and hear the jokes and wisecracks, and relive the excitement of your trip time and time again. After watching today's action, I'm ready to book again for next year."

So the next time you find yourself in the office, swamped by work and mired in deadlines, stop and remember those lucky few indulging in the ultimate fishing experience known as Bristol Bay. But don't think too hard about all the fish they'll be catching. If the siren song gets to you, at least wait until you can make a reservation on the next flight north. It's a long, long walk to Alaska.

Planning Your Trip

WHEN TO GO

The Wood River-Togiak drainages offer excellent sockeye fishing in June, king fishing in July, silver fishing in August and September, and pink and chum salmon in July and August. Rainbow, grayling, pike, Dolly Varden, arctic char and lake trout are available year-round.

WHAT TO TAKE

Although tackle is provided at most of the full-service lodges, many anglers prefer to bring their favorite rods and equipment. In addition, take along waders/hip boots, sunglasses, camera and warm clothing, as well as summer wear for those scorcher days, where temperatures can reach into the high 80s.

HOW TO GET THERE

Take commercial airlines to Dillingham. There, lodge personnel will meet you upon arrival.

WHERE TO STAY

Lodges in the area offer complete services, as well as outpost camps for anglers who wish to pursue individual species. There are presently over 75 lodges in the Bristol Bay region.

APPROXIMATE COST

Full-service lodges in this area average $4,000 per person for a 7-day stay. Four-day packages are available, as are lodges that offer fewer services for less money.

WHO TO CONTACT

For a listing of guides, outfitters and do-it-yourself services, turn to page 208, "Free Information to Plan Your Trip."

12 Adventure

Seals and sea lions are common sights when halibut fishing out of Seward or Valdez.

Flat Island Flatfish

AFTER 30 YEARS OF FISHING, Ken Lomax was finally in the right place at the right time. He had hooked his trophy fish. Yet after 15 minutes, the prognosis was not good.

Heavy beads of sweat hung over Lomax's furrowed brow. His knuckles were chalky white with tension from his vise-like grip on the rod. The situation was approaching critical.

Reshuffling his feet for a better foothold, he summoned all his remaining strength and threw his 160 pounds into the rod. But whatever he had hooked didn't move. Instead, the rod was slowly being pulled from his grasp.

Again he leveraged his weight against the fish, trying to budge what was undoubtedly a stubborn fish of gargantuan size 180 feet below him. The rod creaked under the pressure once. Twice. Three times. Lomax was gaining ground. The tip rose a few inches and prompted a smile on his taught face.

But the euphoria was short lived. The fish came to life, and surged into the depths, nearly pulling Lomax over the railing.

"It's gotta be at least 150 pounds," he said, grunting to keep the rod off the gunwales. "With my luck, it's probably an ol' killer whale or somethin'."

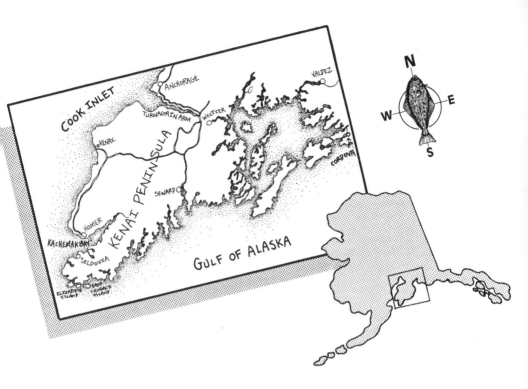

We were destined never to find out. Seconds later, the pressure and surging quit without warning. The line hung limp, and the fish of a lifetime, gone. Disappointment hung heavy in the air. But Lomax felt another "tap-tap" at the end of his line. His interest again sparked, he responded with a hook-set.

Dishing out only a fraction of the power Lomax had felt earlier, the fish surged and fought boldly. The drag screeched, and the rod bucked and fluttered. At first, it was too close to call, but Lomax soon started to gain ground. Twenty minutes later, guide David Coray let the gaff fly into a 30-pound halibut.

"This definitely wasn't the big fish you first hooked," Coray said, "but it is a respectable fish. There are plenty more where this one came from. Last year, we hooked a 129-pounder from this very spot, and plenty of 50-pounders. Just keep fishing."

Lomax didn't need any more coaxing. He had a taste of Alaska halibut fishing, and he began to fish hard for another round with what he now referred to as "Mr. Big."

Although trout aficionados often term Alaska halibut fishing as, "A jerk at one end waiting for a jerk on the other," pay them no mind. A strike from a halibut is often much more than a jerk. It's a signal that starts a rough-and-tumble bout that has few equals, and for good reason.

An Alaska-grown Pacific halibut is a super heavyweight slugger with a division and honor all its own. For instance, the fish has stamina beyond belief. Adults can travel more than 2,000 miles and to depths of 600 or more fathoms. They've also been known to sink boats, break arms and legs and snap 80-pound Dacron as if it were sewing thread.

Despite its power, such a fish isn't born ready to do battle. Rather, its beginnings are meek and mysterious, one that is aptly suited for the lifestyle Mother Nature gave it.

Pacific halibut spawn between November and March along the continental shelf. A female will lay anywhere from two to three million eggs annually. After the eggs hatch, they become free-floating larvae. Then, ocean currents carry them for hundreds of miles along the Pacific Northwest coast.

During the next six months, an astonishing change takes place. The larvae's fish-like form begins to flatten, and its left eye migrates to its right side. At this time, juvenile halibut migrate to shallow water to begin their bottom-feeding lifestyle.

In the halibut family, the females call the shots. Female halibut are larger than male halibut, weighing up to 500 pounds and living 35 to 45 years. On the other hand, males rarely exceed 40 pounds and live a maximum of 25 years. Also, female halibut are more numerous than males. The current Alaska record for a sport-caught halibut is a 450-pound fish. However, most sport-caught halibut average around 30 pounds. The State of Alaska recognizes any halibut over 200 pounds as a trophy, and offers anglers lucky enough to catch one a handsome, parchment certificate attesting to their feat.

In years past, anglers traveling to Alaska were intent on only fishing her blue-ribbon trout and salmon waters. They wouldn't consider spending an extra few days fishing for halibut. Now, if you haven't planned at least a two-day side trip fishing for halibut, you're not playing with a full deck of fish.

Homer halibut charter businesses have been catering to anglers since the sportfishery began in earnest in Alaska sometime in the early 1970s. Much of their business each year is by word of mouth advertising. And there's much to advertise.

The average size of halibut has been increasing. The average weight of sport-caught fish in 1984 was 20.7 pounds. It is now over 27 pounds. Skippers expect even better weights in the future.

"The halibut fishing has been getting better each year," says halibut skipper Mike Huff. "Last year, I guided six anglers to a record, one-day catch of 1,095 pounds.

"Every person on board caught a fish over 100 pounds. One angler hooked two over 100. The largest was 150 pounds, followed by 145, 140, 130, 125, 115 and 110-pounders. The remaining fish weighed in at 40 to 60 pounds."

A fishing guide struggles to hoist up this 300-pound halibut caught in lower Cook Inlet in late July. The fish had to be shot several times before being brought aboard.

Huff said that after the sixth fish, he started to worry about running out of shotshells. To prevent damage to anglers, boat and tackle, it's common for Huff to grab his .410 and shoot all fish over 50 pounds prior to bringing them onboard.

"I didn't expect to dispatch that many fish in one day," he said. "I always try to have a full box of shells whenever I head out.

"There are few other sportfish that offer both fight, size and fine eating. A halibut can yield up to 60 percent of boneless, white fillets. And when the fish is retailing at $4 per pound, anglers are finding that it's not only fun to catch halibut, but also an extremely economical way to fill their freezer with one of the best-tasting fish the Pacific has to offer. Catch a couple of 80 to 100-pounders and you'll have the makings of some fine barbecues to last all summer and most of the winter."

You would be wise to plan early. Halibut charters, however, are available from May through September, but weekends book quickly, as do holidays. You'll also need to make advance reservations for long-range trips, the current trend in halibut sportfishing.

David Coray gaffs a halibut for angler Ken Lomax. Anglers who are familiar with handling boats in the wind and tide-ravaged lower Cook Inlet can do well in small boats, while larger boats are required to reach the trophy halibut grounds near Flat Island.

"For about $25 more, we spend an extra hour traveling and hit the far islands in the Gulf of Alaska," Huff said. "There, halibut stocks are not hammered as hard, and anglers stand a much better chance of catching one or more trophy halibut." He favors areas around Flat and Elizabeth islands, as well as the Barren Islands.

It's rare that Huff, and other charter operators journeying out to the islands, return with fish less than 50 pounds. Most are in the 50 to 100-pound-plus category.

"Of course, keep in mind weather plays a big part in where we can fish," he said. "If we can get out there, and pull in behind an island, chances are we'll have good fishing."

Catching halibut is easy, and takes no specialized tackle or years of expertise. However, attention to detail pays big dividends if you're after the lunkers.

Most skippers use cut herring impaled on a 9/0 or 10/0 hook attached to a slip-sinker rig of 20 to 40 ounces. Huff's clients have also caught big halibut on cod.

"What happens is a cod will bite the herring, and when anglers are pulling it up, a big halibut will take it. They'll bite a fighting cod in an instant.

"You just drop it down there, and jig it a few times," he said. "It's not a matter of whether you'll catch halibut or not. You will. The fish are there."

With a daily bag limit of two fish, anglers are often particular about the size of fish they take home. Most will toss back the smaller fish of 10 and 20 pounds, keeping only the big ones. And there's no questioning when a big halibut grabs it. When you set the hook, the fish pulls back with equal gusto. Then, it's just a matter of getting it to the boat.

I found out as Huff anchored us off a small strip of land near Elizabeth Island in lower Cook Inlet. I was long-lining a six-ounce jig tipped with herring when I couldn't feel either the lure or bottom. I reared back on the rod, felt resistance and reared back again, this time holding the tip high.

The heavy-action rod vibrated wildly. After 20 minutes of tug-o-war, Huff fired a .410 shell into the fish's head, let the gaff fly, and hauled aboard an 84-pounder. Not huge, but plenty of fine eating. Halibut fever had reached epidemic proportions, and the only cure was to continue fishing for these flatfish.

Three days later, I was fishing for halibut with Stan Stephens out of Valdez. It was in mid July, several months after the infamous Exxon Valdez oil spill.

My partner, Jeff Schuler, had never caught a fish larger than a 10-inch trout, and he jumped at the chance to pursue halibut. He also jumped at the chance to catch the first fish. When an 89-pound halibut nailed his herring and proceeded to nearly pull him over the railing, it was all I could do to keep the tears of laughter away. His face was locked in amazement. So was mine, when the halibut surfaced and cleared the water in one jump. I had never seen a halibut perform such a feat in my nearly two decades of fishing Alaska. Schuler went wild, and I stood by ready to grab his coat, just in case he started slipping over the side. After 15 minutes of battle, I gaffed the halibut and brought it aboard. At that moment, there was not a happier angler than Schuler. He decreed that the spill didn't affect the halibut fishing in the least.

I've obtained much of my halibut fishing expertise from experience, as has Nick Dudiak, veteran halibut fisherman and sportfish biologist in Homer. He believes that hootchie or plastic skirts on a baited hook give the angler an added advantage.

"Whether you use scent or bait, the plastic hootchie will pick up and hold that scent for a period of time," Dudiak says. "Thus, if the halibut steals the bait, the skirt will have enough fish oil on it to draw another strike. Without the skirt, the angler would be fishing a bare hook."

Dudiak catches halibut on a regular basis by incorporating vibration, visual appeal and scent. He's had very good success fishing a large spinner/hootchie combo off a lead weight. When baited with a herring/hootchie combo mentioned earlier, the rig pulsates along bottom, and big halibut "really smash it," he said.

While I've caught my share of halibut on herring, I've also had excellent success with 8 to 14-ounce, nickel-plated Krocodile, Vi-ke or Diamond jigs. For me, an up-and-down, erratic jigging technique several feet above bottom has been an excellent producer of big halibut over the years. A piece of squid on the hook seems to also increase the effectiveness of the lure.

Opposite page: Halibut fishing often provides your money's worth of adventure. Donned in a survival suit, the boat's first mate is lowered into Cook Inlet to cut the anchor rope the skipper had entangled in the boat's prop. Meanwhile the boat tilted dangerously on its side in the receding tide, forcing evacuation of the boat. Eventually the boat and deckhand made it safely back to port.

At left: Tomahawk skipper Mike Huff helps Chris Batin hoist up an 84-pound halibut.

Here's another tip passed on to me by sportfish biologist Durand Cook: He believes the white belly skin of halibut is an extremely effective attractor when fishing either bait or lures. I've tried it, and agree. It equals the more expensive pork rind I have used in the past. Best of all, it's free. Freeze your skins after a day's fishing, and save them for future trips.

If you're determined to catch big halibut, you can't go wrong by using a big bait. Veteran halibut anglers will use an entire salmon head impaled on a No. 10 hook and fished within 15 feet of the bottom during slack tide, a time when big halibut are on the feed. Rarely does this rig produce anything smaller than 100-pound fish.

Why Cook Inlet and Prince William Sound as my top choices for halibut? Accessibility. Most anglers fishing western Alaska, Bristol Bay or southcentral are within flying or driving distance of these fisheries. It's no extra hassle for anglers to spend an extra day or two on a charter boat, catch the sights and some fine eating fish. This opportunity especially appeals to catch-and-release trout and salmon fishermen, who would otherwise return home with little or no fish for their freezers.

In addition to halibut, fishing for rockfish and lingcod is also available in these areas, with Seward and Valdez taking top honors as the most popular destinations for these two species.

Before I forget, Kodiak Island and Southeast Alaska also offers excellent halibut fishing. If your itinerary calls for a stop at one or more of Southeast's coastal cities, you'd be wise to book at least

While fishing for halibut, the author photographed these inquisitive Orca kiler whales. They stopped directly beneath the boat, turned sideways and looked upwards for several seconds before moving on.

one trip. My favorite halibut fisheries are Ketchikan's Prince of Wales and Revilla islands, and the waters near Petersburg. But don't exclude Juneau, Yakutat and Sitka, which offer halibut fishing on par with the rest of the state.

Halibut may not be the prettiest fish in the world, nor are they the most aesthetic in terms of technique or acquired skill, but they are loads of fun and great eating. To coin a phrase, "Why ask for anything more?"

Planning Your Trip

WHEN TO GO

May through September is an excellent time for halibut fishing. In mid summer, there's up to 19 hours of daylight for fishing. Weather can reach in the mid to upper 70s or low 80s, and don't forget the salmon fishing action also available throughout the summer.

WHAT TO TAKE

A day-long charter trip lasts from 8 to 12 hours. Take along a lunch, raingear, deck shoes and hat with visor. If you're prone to sea sickness, purchase Dramamine or better yet, acquire a prescription from your doctor for scopolamine ear patches. One patch lasts for up to three days and is extremely effective in combating sea sickness. Sunglasses are also necessary, as are Zip-loc bags and a filet knife to process and package your fish at day's end.

While most boats provide gear, I suggest you take your own. Choose a heavy-action seven-foot boat rod and a large-capacity, level-wind reel filled with at least 300 feet of 80 to 120-pound Dacron line. A slip-sinker rig using one or two 20-ounce weights (depending on tidal flow), and a 300-pound test ball-bearing swivel will put you in business. Size 10/0 Tru-Turn hooks are a favorite hook for hooking large fish, and I prefer these over the circle hooks. Runner up is a standard J-hook. For anglers who are unfamiliar with the soft strike of a halibut, circle hooks offer better chances for a hook-up. Metal and leadhead jigs from 6 to 16 ounces work well during slack tide.

HOW TO GET THERE

Homer, Seward and Valdez are accessible via highway or air. If you're driving to Alaska, and are trailering your own boat, you can find good halibut fishing in Cook Inlet. Stop at the Deep Creek Wayside, Mile 138 Sterling Highway. Fish the area about three miles out from Happy Valley or Twin Falls. For big halibut, search for channels in 120 feet of water. These structures attract halibut migrating in from deeper water. Drift with the current while bottom bouncing herring, squid or other bait. Carry and use an anchor should you find that hotspot. A word of warning: Cook Inlet winds can kick up in minutes, so ensure your 25-horse or larger motor can get you to shore without delay. This is a potentially dangerous fishery, so use caution!

WHERE TO STAY

Accommodations are available along the coast as well as remote areas. Various lodges and outfitters offer a variety of packages from which to choose. An excellent alternative is to charter a boat for several days. Once you're out on the fishing grounds, you can fish for as long as you like. It's possible to catch and release halibut, keeping only the larger fish for the freezer.

APPROXIMATE COSTS

Day charters are the most common, and available in most all of Alaska's major coastal cities. They run about $125 per day per person. Special long-range day trips cost from $125 to $150, depending on the area fished. On long-range trips, a first-class charter operator will offer a luxury motor yacht or boat, sleeping accommodations for at least six, fishing gear, meals, rain gear, small boat for shore excursions, skipper and first mate for about $700 per day, four-person minimum, six-person maximum.

WHO TO CONTACT

For a listing of guides, outfitters and do-it-yourself services, turn to page 208, "Free Information to Plan Your Trip."

13 Adventure

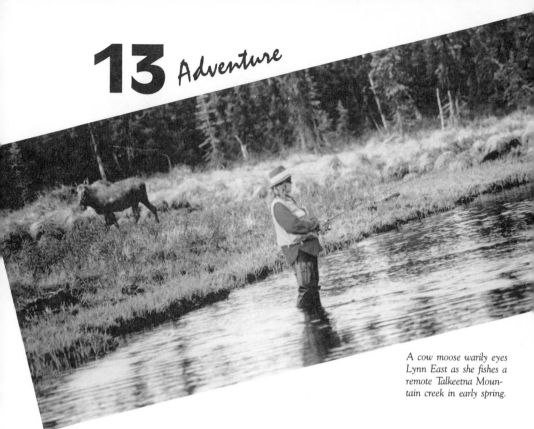

A cow moose warily eyes Lynn East as she fishes a remote Talkeetna Mountain creek in early spring.

Talkeetna's Rainbow Splendor

I HAVE SEEN GREATER STREAMS in the Pacific Northwest, ones whose dam-fed waters roared with authority as trout anglers probed their depths with lead-core fly lines and bulky muddlers. But this mountain, snow-melt trickle of water I was fishing was the antithesis of those giants; a gentle pulse of a stream whose lifeblood was the steady drip-drip of melting snow from a nearby bank.

Overall, the stream was comely. It had no textbook features that prompted a trout fisherman to envision pot-bellied rainbows holding beneath its current. Up from the water's edge, limbs of intertwining sub-arctic willows and birch, not yet budded from the cold spring, spread their limbs like a trap to catch the first trespasser. Yet there was something about this stream's delicate nature that sensitized my being. My philosophy is, "Fish a stream and experience it to its fullest."

I complied by laying out a perfect cast. Anticipation gave way to excitement. The strike was instantaneous. Every nerve ending came alive.

And feel I did, with every part of my soul. These were no ordinary rainbows, but Darwin's progeny, the survival of the fittest.

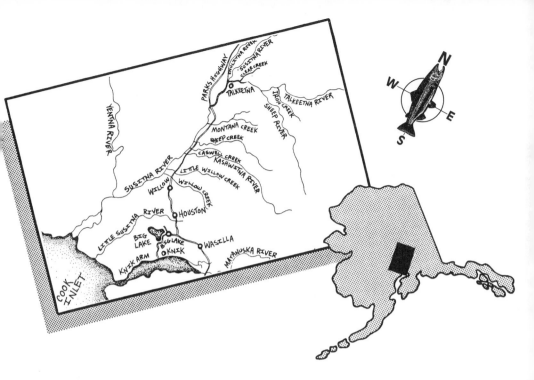

They were rainbows on their spawning run; Alaska wild rainbows, the kind that leap in aerial contortions that is poetry in motion, and radiate a spectrum of colors that artists envy.

Minutes later, I slowly led the rainbow to my hand that trembled not from the cold, but from the anticipatory thrill of encountering such a wild and wonderful fish.

The icy, scaled flesh numbed my hand as I mentally probed the fish with my fingertips. I visually absorbed everything about this fish to verify what my eyes were relaying. The trout's gill plates were like a bellows, opening and closing in slow, rhythmic patterns that fanned the glowing magenta ember emblazoned on the fish's side.

I slowly lowered this living palette of colors into the water. With a snap of its tail, the rainbow disappeared into the muskeg-stained depths of the tundra pool. I crouched on the bank and suffered from mixed feelings: sad that I couldn't admire the fish for a longer period of time, yet joyful that it would continue to propagate its species.

Nearby, friends Doug and Lynn East were catching rainbows with nearly every cast.

"Come on down and fish this spot," Doug called out. "They're everywher... ," his voice trailing off as he set the hook into another rainbow.

"No thanks," I said, taking a seat in a small opening on the bank. "I'm doing fine right here."

Opposite page: Guide Jim Bailey with a vibrantly-striped spring rainbow in full spawning colors. Using a standard egg pattern, Bailey caught other rainbows holding behind a school of spawning suckers.

At left: Sports Afield editor Jay Cassell reacts quickly to the acrobatics of this Talkeetna rainbow. It's common for stream-caught rainbows to jump two to three feet at the hookset.

There was something reverent about catching so many rainbows at this time of year: Something, maybe, that other anglers didn't fully appreciate.

My guide Jim Bailey walked over through the knee-high brush and sat on a nearby patch of Labrador tea. A man who is extremely sensitive to the resource, Bailey considers it a privilege to pursue springtime rainbows. Yet his first and foremost concern is with the fish's well-being.

"That fish get off o.k.?" he questioned.

"Oh, sure. Spunky and full of fight," I replied.

Bailey, too, appreciates this special breed of fish, and like a handful of others I know, relishes fishing at this time of year. As we munched on a few chocolate chip cookies I had stashed in my vest pocket, Bailey openly discussed this remarkable fishery.

"The rainbow action is exceptional only a few weeks out of each year," he said. "In the spring, the rainbows are on their spawning run, and are congregated in large numbers at just a few locations throughout this drainage. After spawning, many are ravenous and will hit just about anything. This feeding frenzy lasts for as long as a day to several weeks. Then the rainbows disappear into the lakes and rivers, where they are relatively tough to catch until late summer and autumn."

Bailey went on to say that many streams in southcentral Alaska are closed to fishing for rainbows in early spring, and for good

In the Talkeetnas, water conditions vary from year to year, creating for unpredictable fishing conditions. Overall, anglers wearing neoprene waders fare best in the cold, snow-melt streams.

reason. For instance, in years past, the Kenai River's rainbow population was severely depleted due to liberal bag limits and overharvesting. Luckily, the population is starting to bounce back. But here, nestled in valleys of the Talkeetna Mountains, premier rainbow fishing can still be had at its fullest. And Jim Bailey, the only full-time guide in this area, isn't about to allow anyone to harm this resource.

"Anglers need to use single, barbless hooks. And there is no keeping fish. Fiberglass mounts are the preferred trophy. Simple rules make for outstanding fishing," he concluded.

It was 10 p.m., and the orange, summer sun held low in the northern sky. Rainbows and grayling inhaled our fly presentations with the same zest they had exhibited that morning. There was only one difference: fatigue had finally set in for the anglers. But it was a type of fatigue that invigorates the senses rather than numbs them, one that contributes to treasured memories of fish caught and released, in company with others who share the same philosophy.

Later that night, after a full-course meal, the figures were confirmed: Over 125 rainbow trout caught within two days, most measuring from 18 to 26 inches. We tallied up the figures again to be sure. We were wrong. We had caught 143 rainbows, with 78 taken on sculpin and smolt patterns, the rest on ultralight spinning gear.

Doug tore out from his notepad the piece of paper with the figures and handed it to Bailey, who shook his head in mock disbelief.

"Yep, I just don't know where to find the rainbows this year," he joked in a serious monotone. "This late spring has everything all changed around."

Later in the season, Talkeetna rainbows often lose their dark red coloration, yet still maintain a fairly bright pinkish hue and coal-black markings.

"If this is poor fishing, I better not indulge further," I said as I examined my ravaged, hairless supply of once-beautifully tied streamers. Even the dry flies, used to entice and catch grayling as well as rainbows, teetered on wobbly strands of chewed hackle.

"It's so a guy can't afford to go fishing, as hard as these fish are on flies," I said. "I'm just happy we don't have to walk to the fishing hole from here."

Reaching these isolated streams is not an easy task when the major access route is the Talkeetna River, a gutsy type of waterway that is not for the faint of heart. Logjams resemble medieval gargoyles, stretching their tentacle-like snags over milky glacial waters to ensnare the careless boater. Float plane pilots find many sections of the river too hazardous to attempt a landing. Yet when the Tanaina Indians named the river "Talkeetna" meaning "river of plenty," they weren't referring to the "plenty of problems" associated with access and travel on the river. Rather, the name refers to thousands of salmon, char, grayling and trout that migrate up this waterway and its many clearwater tributaries from late May through September.

Steve Mahay, owner of Mahay's Riverboat Service in Talkeetna, knows the Talkeetna rainbow as good if not better than anyone. He has been directly responsible for showing me many of the wonders of the Talkeetna River fishery.

"The majority of the rainbows anglers catch range from 14 to 21 inches," he said. "Occasionally, someone will catch a 27-inch-plus fish. Also, the riverboat trip to the various rainbow holes is exciting."

That's a general understatement. Expect some fancy boat

145

handling dodging snags and sweepers, and a chance to view wildlife such as black bear, brown bear and moose.

Angler Tim Hagerty of New Hampshire recently fished the Talkeetna for the first time. An avid fly fisher who has traveled across the North American continent in search of rainbows, Hagerty says the trout fishing he experienced on a small Talkeetna stream was some of the best he's had. "I hooked as many as 15 rainbows in one afternoon, and had that many get off," he said. "It was great fishing."

Despite the superb angling, the Talkeetna receives more publicity about its salmon fisheries than its rainbow riches. One reason is access. Salmon streams are easily accessible along the mainstem Susitna and lower Talkeetna, while the rainbows require a lengthy riverboat journey or fly-in via floatplane.

Another is effort. The good rainbow fishing I've experienced each year is more than a cast off the side of the boat at the Dolly Hole. Expect to hike several miles, through brush and along bear trails, to reach the best rainbow fishing. I assure you, the rewards are worth the effort of keeping in shape.

For example, consider two trips I made last year. On the first, with angler Mark Wade, I hooked and released 52 rainbows, grayling and char, all from a 20-foot stretch of river. The largest went six pounds, and the bow's girth was wider than the distance between the tips of my little finger and my thumb.

Later in the season, I joined Tim Hagerty on a three-mile hike through brush, swamp and forest, and fished a tiny gem of a stream. We caught 32 fish, the largest being a 27-inch rainbow that terrorized my 6-weight fly rod. That catch was pure joy.

Fishing was easy. We would leap frog past each other, fishing various holding structures such as rocks, riffles, logjams and pools; classic textbook trout water that generates a feeling of anticipation which disappears with the first jump of the strike indicator. Best of all, we didn't see another angler on the upper stretch. Allow me to clarify. About a mile from the mouth, we did confront a brown bear. I first spotted him standing on a fallen tree in mid river, looking for fish. Suddenly, he jumped onto the bank and started walking our way.

I grabbed Tim's arm and jumped into the shallows. We wasted no time fording the creek. As we walked out onto the gravel on the opposite shore, the bear stood up, saw us, woofed once, and ran into the brush.

"That brownie was a good eight feet tall!" Tim exclaimed. "I'm sure glad you had your gun ready."

"What gun?" I countered.

Later that afternoon, I talked with Mahay about the possibilities

Brown bears are plentiful along many Talkeetna tributaries. Avoid conflicts by making noise, especially when walking brushy stream banks.

of fishing the Talkeetna on your own.

He said anglers with their own riverboats can reach upper Talkeetna fisheries, but he offers a word of caution, especially those who are unfamiliar with river travel.

"The Talkeetna is an obstacle course, and it takes a special boat to handle the river," he says. "Each summer I see from 10 to 15 so called "riverboats" capsized by logjams or sweepers, and there have been a few fatalities. All it takes is a power failure or a miscalculated turn, and the current will smash you into a log jam. Unless the sides of your boat are 30 inches or higher, you'll take on water and go under.

"Even if a person is careful, there is always the unexpected. For instance, sleepers—water-soaked logs that can weigh up to several tons—can suddenly pop to the surface and flip a boat or punch a hole through the hull. Also, debris from high water and glacial silt can block the intake of a jet and send a boat floating helplessly toward a series of sweepers. It's a dangerous river, and anglers should use a boat that's either capable of handling the river, or else charter with one of the riverboat operators in the area."

Mahay uses heavy-duty riverboats that weigh up to 3.5 tons. They have 3/16-inch marine aluminum sides and a 1/4-inch bottom. Tests show that a .38 caliber pistol fired at point-blank range will not penetrate the hull. Two boats are 24-footers with 34-inch sides, and the other is a 27-footer with an eight-foot beam and 40-inch sides. All are powered by 454 Chevy big-block, high-performance engines that churn out over 300 horsepower to operate a seven-inch jet unit. (For the uninitiated, a jet unit is a propulsion system that uses an impeller to suck up water, much like a jet engine sucks in air, and thrusts it out at high speed. This allows for fast travel over gravel bars with a water depth of only inches, a common occurrence on the Talkeetna.)

Despite the logistics required to reach these streams, expect crowds at popular areas such as Clear Creek. Crowds are intense during holidays, especially the July 4th weekend when several hundred people may line the stream bank. At this time of year, Mahay says his boats stay running 16 hours per day.

I spent the few remaining days on the upper Talkeetna tributary walking sections of stream. A cast into a pool or behind a rock oftentimes produced a slashing strike, or a particularly colorful rainbow with large, charcoal-black spots. Catching these fish is always exciting. At times, certain sections of stream seemed void of fish. However, I welcomed such stretches, not only because they allowed me time to rest a tired arm, but also to reflect upon how lucky I was to be fishing for wild, 18-inch-plus rainbows with a light fly rod in a non-stressful angling environment in the Alaska wilds.

Indeed, riverboating adventure and fantastic rainbow, trout and char fishing is what the Talkeetna River system is all about. Take the time to properly plan your trip, check your equipment, don't take risks, and expect to have a great time. You won't be disappointed.

Planning Your Trip

WHEN TO GO

In the lower drainages, good rainbow fishing can be enjoyed, when regulations allow, in early May. At higher elevations, streams don't ice-out until early to mid June. Always call the charter service or lodge before departing to ensure lakes and streams are open, and that the waters are not muddy from spring ice melt. Certain closures apply to fishing for rainbow trout in various watersheds. Check with the Alaska Department of Fish and Game for specific information.

WHAT TO TAKE

Smolt patterns in sizes 4 through 6, egg sucking leeches and muddler patterns work best, as do size 2 and 3 spinners with silver or gold blades. On bright days, try a woolly bugger or zug bug, especially on fish holding in deep holes. Dry flies include black gnat, yellow humpy, Adams, Chena renegade and mosquito. Flyrodders should use 4 to 6-weight rods, six-foot sink tip and/or floating line. Take split shot or wrap-on lead for the deeper runs and pools.

Best lures include Mepps 00 spinners or 1/8-ounce single-hook spoons in silver/blue. Or if you have an ultralight rod and two-pound test line, try drifting pink or red Glo-Bugs with a piece of shot 12 to 24 inches up the line.

Talkeetna and Susitna River tributaries are snag paradises. Bring twice as many flies and lures as you need, and even then, an extra handful. You'll also lose plenty on wild fish and on the abrasive, gravely bottom.

HOW TO GET THERE

Drive to Talkeetna, which is located about 225 miles south of Fairbanks, or 125 miles north of Anchorage. A public boat ramp and campground is available. Various lodges offer pre-season fishing discounts. Shop around for the best price.

WHERE TO STAY

Overnight accommodations are available in Talkeetna. Most anglers prefer to leave the day of their arrival, spending the night near the fishing area. Early spring can be wet and rainy, so be prepared with proper raingear, tents and tarps.

APPROXIMATE COSTS

The least expensive rainbow fishing trip will run about $50 to $100 per person, while a lodge room, meals and fishing can run from $110 to $300 per day.

WHO TO CONTACT

For a listing of guides, outfitters and do-it-yourself services, turn to page 208, "Free Information To Plan Your Trip."

14 Adventure

The upper Aniak River float is one of the wildest and most rugged fishing adventure floats in Alaska.

Fishing the Aniak: An Adventure for the Strong of Heart

THE ANIAK RIVER is not what would be considered a textbook Alaska trout stream. Logjams the size of houses block the river, making navigation possible for only the most experienced guide.

The river itself has a chameleon complexion; one day it's clear, the next brown from heavy rains, then green from mid summer algae growth. The Aniak's tributaries are the color of strong tea and offer hiding spots for fat rainbow trout and pike that gorge on an abundance of terrestrials. You don't walk to the fishing: you take a kayak and squirm around sweepers, or hop into a Super Cub aircraft and bounce to a stop on a remote gravel bar.

The river changes each year, providing for unique and challenging fishing opportunities. Indeed, anglers wanting one of the best mixed-bag fisheries in Alaska sportfishing, along with what is perhaps one of the most unusual yet adventurous sport fisheries available, will find the Aniak a river to quench the most feverish angling desires.

Don't try to fish the Aniak on your own; it can be done, but

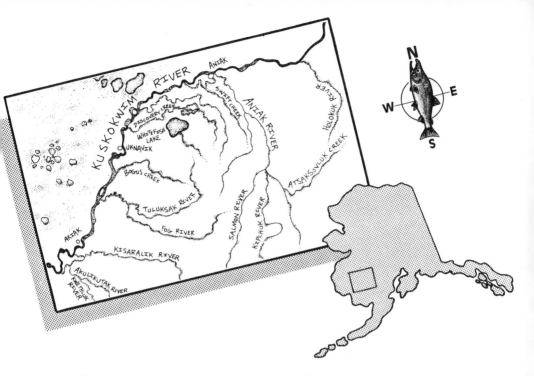

generally it's a lesson in futility and extremely dangerous in spots. To properly fish the area requires an extensive inventory of equipment, especially if your quarry is fly rod king salmon or darkly spotted, "leopard 'bows" to seven-pounds.

There are several ways to reach the fishing on the Aniak, and where you want to fish will dictate the means of travel. You'll require Super Cub aircraft with huge tundra tires to access the remote stretches, and inflatables to float those stretches; jet-equipped riverboats for fast access to headwater sloughs in the lower river; canoes or folding kayaks to ease through the sloughs and access the deep pools where trout and salmon hold, and a portable base camp to relax in at day's end. This is pure outpost camp fishing, the kind many of us knew years ago on the Goodnews and the Kanektok rivers. One day, the Aniak will be overcrowded, also. But for now, it is crying to be experienced in all its solitude.

At 2,240 square miles, the Aniak drainage is massive enough and far enough away to be termed wilderness. Its headwaters begin a few miles north of the Wood River-Tikchik Lakes State Park in Aniak Lake, and the river flows in a northerly direction. After 100 miles of coursing through a variety of terrain, the river empties into the Kuskokwim River at Aniak. It is here that you'll find the northern and westernmost distribution of rainbow trout in the world. In the Aniak they reach their farthest limit of distribution.

The Aniak fishery is perhaps the best-kept rainbow secret in western Alaska. Because of adverse conditions and difficulty of

151

access, many do-it-yourself anglers and guides won't consider fishing there. But the Aniak River contains more rainbow trout than other streams in this area. Depending on time of year, you'll also catch all five species of Pacific salmon plus char, grayling, whitefish, pike and sheefish.

In the lower 10 miles of river, where it merges with the Kuskokwim, the Aniak is a mud-banked, silty river stretching in places to over 200 feet wide. The surrounding vegetation consists of dense stands of spruce, birch, aspen, alder and willows. Whitefish and ciscoes, along with sheefish, like holding in nearby sloughs and oxbows formed by the river's meandering. The best time to catch these species is in early spring, immediately after ice-out (early to mid May). Also, northern pike fishing is generally excellent in Dead End Slough and Grassy Slough. Both areas also offer some char and grayling fishing.

The terrain and river bottom changes above Doestock Creek. Bottom composition is 10 percent silt and sand, 30 percent fine gravel, 40 percent medium gravel and 20 percent coarse gravel. This section is nightmarish to run in a riverboat, due to the many trees and logjams throughout this section. Anglers can expect current flowing at four to five feet per second, greater in high water. In this section, numerous sloughs enter the river and create deep pools, which are prime locations for catching rainbow trout and char.

Also try fishing at the slough mouths themselves. There you'll find an abundance of aquatic invertebrates. Dry fly fishing or nymph fishing is very effective here for chunky rainbows, grayling and smallish char. Farther up in the sloughs, expect fair to good pike fishing for fish from three to 10 pounds. Mouse patterns, streamers and poppers are all effective.

A word about the Doestock. Smolt patterns are most effective in catching rainbow, char, grayling and pike from mid to late May. A few sheefish in the five to 15 pound range can be caught on spoons and large attractor patterns. Surveys show that sheefish are not found past the Doestock.

For excellent rainbow trout, char, grayling, whitefish and northern pike fishing, try from Mile 16 through 18. How good is the rainbow fishing? On one day, when water conditions were good, we each caught 14 between 21 and 27 inches. Best time is late June through ice-up.

If you have access to a boat during periods of high water, the Buckstock is a choice location. The river is fed by run-off from surrounding tundra. Depending on time of year, expect either brown or green-stained water. Deep pools and riffles alternate along this 60-foot-wide river. Willows and alders make fishing from the

J.W. Smith with a king salmon he hooked on ultralight trout gear while float fishing the Aniak drainage. Because sweepers and logjams are plentiful, most fishing is done from shore rather than from a moving boat.

bank an impossibility. Fishing must be done from mid stream via wading or casting to shore from a boat. Resident species hold in the snags and jams lining the bank. King, chum and silver salmon can also be caught in fair to good numbers in the Buckstock in spawning pools and in the major channels.

From the Buckstock River to the Kipchuk River, expect a swift current with an always changing channel. Boating in this stretch is both difficult and dangerous. Gravel bars are numerous, as are log jams and sweepers. However, the many deep pools and runs provide ideal holding habitat for rainbows, salmon and char. Running upriver in a jetboat through this section gets the adrenalin pumping because real danger exists. But the reward is worth it. Most of the king and chum salmon entering this stretch spawn in the Salmon and nearby Timber Creek. Anglers can expect several thousand salmon to be available each year, more than one can possibly fish for in a week's time. Sight casting flies such as flashabous, king killers and Baker busters to large kings is the norm, and the hook-up rate is 20 to 50 percent. Don't take anything less than a 10-weight rod with plenty of spine.

The only way to reach the upper Aniak is via Super Cub aircraft landing on various gravel bars. Don't confuse this trip with those found in the lower river, and accessible by powerboats.

The Salmon River provides a sand/gravel bottom, and offers good fishing within the first three miles from its confluence with the Aniak. Salmon fishing is excellent, with the best fishing taking place from the mouth to Marvel Creek. The area is also a prime location for rainbow trout fishing, especially in mid May. Fish are plentiful because this stretch of the river provides ideal overwintering habitat. As spring and summer progress, these fish move into the feeder tributaries and streams. However, keep in mind that despite the good rainbow fishing, your success depends on water clarity, which is influenced by rainfall and temperature.

The Salmon, along with the nearby Kipchuk, also offers good fishing in August for stocky rainbow and grayling.

Aniak Lake

Due to low water throughout spring and summer, access to Aniak Lake from Aniak River is not possible. However, it is definitely worth fishing for the fly-in angler who has access to an inflatable boat.

The lake is in a remarkably scenic location, surrounded by mountains to 4,500 feet elevation. Grayling are plentiful in the lake, and lake trout fishing is good to excellent with fish in the 20-pound-plus range, but most range from four to 14 pounds. Depending on time of year (with spring and fall best) expect from four to 20 fish per hour.

In a nearby lake, anglers will see the remains of two crashed airplanes, a grim reminder that you can make no mistakes when flying in this country.

There are easier watersheds to fish in Alaska, but few offer the challenge and excitement of incorporating adventure/survival skills with superb fishing opportunities. The Aniak is a river for the bold at heart. Challenge it this year and see for yourself.

Planning Your Trip

WHEN TO GO

Best season is from mid June through mid September for rainbow trout, northern pike, grayling, char and lake trout. Try June and July for king and chum salmon; August for pink and coho salmon.

WHAT TO TAKE

The Aniak is not a float for the inexperienced angler or river floater. It's best to book with one of several guides or river float operators before tackling this watershed on your own.

On a guided trip, take neoprene waders, 4, 6 and 8-weight fly rods with both floating and sinking lines for each, as well as mini lead heads. Personal survival gear should be carried at all times, in case you are separated from the group or overturn your craft. Patch or repair kits for waders and hip boots are a must, due to the snag infested waters of the Aniak. Temperatures can reach the 70s and low 80s, but take a jacket and sweater for the cool nights, which can dip into the 40s.

HOW TO GET THERE

Commercial airlines fly to Aniak from Anchorage. Round-trip fare is approximately $500. Access to the fishery is by riverboat or fly-out via local air charter service. Fly-outs average $550 per person.

WHERE TO STAY

Float operators offer temporary camps, or you can camp on your own on numerous gravel bars. Always camp on high ground, as a heavy rainfall can cause a flash flood, washing away your camp in the middle of the night. A handful of lodges operate boats on the main rivers, but rarely reach the upper stretches of area tributaries where rainbow fishing is best.

APPROXIMATE COSTS

This is a wilderness fishery, and the logistics change from year to year, depending on the availability of aircraft and gear rental businesses. Cost for a fully equipped camp, aircraft access, boats, food and flight to and from camp cost $2,600. Do-it-yourself trips run as low as a third of this cost.

WHO TO CONTACT

For a listing of guides, outfitters and do-it-yourself services, turn to page 208, "Free Information to Plan Your Trip."

Of the five species of Pacific salmon in the Grand Slam, fresh sockeyes are the most difficult to hook, followed closely by fresh chum salmon, pictured here.

15 *Adventure*

Grand Slam Salmon of Southwest Alaska

ALASKA SALMON ARE NOT WIMPY strains of *Oncorhynchus* that, like some hatchery fish, have been nurtured and protected throughout their early life. Alaska creates super salmon; macho, streamlined forms whipped into shape by evolutionary adaptation to a wilderness environment. The result is a fish anglers wait a lifetime to experience, a fish that doesn't quit. They'll fight for an hour, and still fight with head-shaking fury at the net. They will jump out of nets and off gaffs, and oftentimes, knock down anglers in the process. This inbred will to survive—imparted by lives nurtured in Alaska's wilderness bosom, rather than in some concrete hatchery—is what makes these salmon the champs of North American sportfish.

Alaska salmon are marathon swimmers, exhibiting unbelievable stamina. They can swim 18 miles a day, non-stop, against 10 m.p.h. river currents, or make a 2,000-mile journey to their spawning grounds in less than 120 days. A human would be lucky if he could walk a mile in such a current.

If you're immune to such reactions due to an allegiance to bass

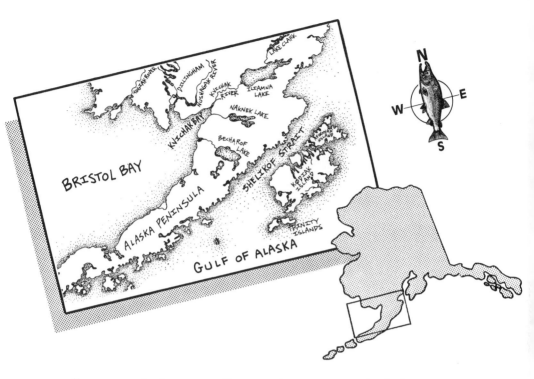

or walleye, a word of warning. Once you've experienced Alaska's
Grand Slam salmon angling, that is catching all five species of
salmon in one trip, other types of sportfishing will never be the
same.

Picture it: one minute you're standing on a crowded stream with
hundreds of other anglers, casting for 12-inch walleye or bass. Smog
stains the southern sky, beer cans float by, and you've yet to see
that first fish being caught.

In less than a day you can be in southwest Alaska, which is
salmon fishing's Garden of Eden, and the reigning home of the
Grand Slam. Such an undertaking is for those who have
transcended ordinary angling adventures. It's for anglers who want
the best of the best.

You'll not find a better place for a Grand Slam than southwest
Alaska. This 54,700-square-mile area includes all waters and
drainages flowing into Bristol Bay, from the Alaska Peninsula to
waters stretching up to Kuskokwim Bay. Expect to cast into a
school of several hundred pink salmon as they push into intertidal
streams. Become crazed with bone-tiring delight as you muscle a
king salmon out of its deep-river hole, or shout with glee over the
cartwheeling acrobatics of a sockeye salmon. Chums will keep you
busy with bulldog runs up and down stream, while cohos will steal
the show with lure-crunching strikes that sometimes strip gears in

157

Jim Oatfield with a sockeye salmon caught on a tributary of the Togiak River. Once they establish their spawning territories, sockeyes are relatively easy to catch.

Opposite page: Walt Panchyshyn quickly realizes this king salmon is far from being beat. While most Slams take place in southwest Alaska, Susitna River tributaries in mid August have yielded numerous slams for anglers.

the best of fly reels. Alaska salmon anglers often count on gear failing as a means of taking a break. Otherwise, they'd fish themselves into oblivion.

Timing is critical in planning your Grand Slam. Because Alaska's salmon runs occur at peak times throughout the summer, it's necessary to find both a place and time when all five species will be in or near a watershed. Ironically, most watersheds only offer two to four species at any one time. More species are often available, but these are often in closed waters, or closed seasons prevent the taking of fish.

Western Bristol Bay, the Mulchatna and the Alaska Peninsula are my personal choices for pursuing a Grand Slam. These regions offer not only the opportunity to catch all five species of salmon, but also provide the numbers of fish, wilderness environment and a variety of fishing situations appropriate for a Grand Slam undertaking. In most cases, you can catch all five species in less than a week.

When is the best time? My favorite has been the third week in August. You start out catching kings, sockeyes, chums and pinks that are already in the streams. By the time an angler catches these four, the first silvers of the year will be entering the same watersheds.

The Alaska Peninsula's location is the principal factor that makes it the ideal choice for a slam. In some areas, the width of the peninsula stretches only 25 miles from the Pacific to the Bering

Sea. Pacific side streams receive their fish one to two weeks before the Bering side. This offers just enough overlap where anglers can catch late-run kings and sockeyes from the Bering, along with fresh-run silvers, chums and pinks from the Pacific. In Bristol Bay, you'll need an airplane to reach the upper headwaters of various rivers such as the Togiak and Kanektok to catch sockeyes and late-run kings, and access to the lower stretch for the best chum, pink and early silver fishing.

When flying over some streams at about 1,000 feet, the water appears to be running muddy along the edges. A drop of the plane's nose will show the "discoloration" to be thousands of salmon, fresh in from the ocean. They pack together for the mad push to the upper headwaters in wilderness valleys that are rimmed with volcanoes (on the peninsula), glacial-and spring-melt streams, and glacial-carved amphitheaters that ring hollow from the last great Ice Age.

Salmon are not the only bounty Bristol Bay has to offer. Her natural wonders greatly contribute to the overall experience.

Expect a variety of fishing terrain, from mountainous to saltwater. A typical day will have your pilot flying you to wilderness saltwater beaches strewn with Japanese fishing floats, bear tracks and bits of old boat wrecks. You'll land on river gravelbars where brown bears and eagles are the only competition.

Indeed, bears are also part of the Grand Slam experience. They can appear almost anywhere. At one lodge I stayed at last summer,

right around midnight a brownie entered the camp, causing the camp watchdog, "Bear," to bark up a storm. The guides looked out the window, and seeing nothing, yelled at the dog to be quiet. When Bear kept barking, they looked a bit closer and found a large brown bear eating the dog's food. The next night, another guide saw the same bear steal the dog's dish.

Anglers also have occasional confrontations with the area's bears. I had just landed a respectable 18-pound coho at the mouth of the Dog Salmon River. The fish had broken the hook, and I turned to shore to replace it. Will Tinnesand, a lodge guest from Federal Way, Washington, came over to see the fish, but before he could offer any congratulations, I saw his face draw tight.

"Geeeesh!" he said hoarsely, looking past me.

As I turned, a large brown bear was less than 30 feet away, lumbering toward us with his nose zeroed in on fish. I grabbed my tackle, and cautioned Will to walk slowly back to the boat while keeping his face to the bear. Will's eyes got even wider as I grabbed my salmon and took it with us.

"Leave the damn fish," he hissed.

"So he can associate food with people?" I fired back? "I'm dropping this fish only if he charges us. So keep walking."

In less than 30 seconds we were in the boat, motoring into the river's main current. The sound of the outboard scared the bear into the brush, where he stayed. From there he peeked at us through the bushes.

"I think he still wants your fish," Will said. "Or maybe he just wants to play."

The next day, Will and I fished for sockeyes and char in the upper headwaters of a creek. The char were holding in good numbers immediately behind the salmon. Salmon egg patterns were

Pink salmon often pose the greatest problem to Slam anglers, as the largest schools seldom migrate far from saltwater. Once found, however, they can be enticed with a variety of patterns such as sockeye greens and chartreuse sparkle shrimps.

the only item on the menu. The char wanted them served slightly above the gravel substrate, on a dead drift. A two-egg marabou was an excellent pattern.

Despite the drizzle and wind, the fishing was good, and the catching was astounding. I stopped counting at 40 char, and had released numerous sockeyes, from 8 to 12 pounds, and several chums in the 10-pound range. I had hooked many other salmon on the 4X tippet, which didn't withstand the ravages of the salmon's spawning dentures. Will had done equally as well, and had lost as many fish on the light gear. Nearly all the char were decked out in full spawning colors.

The next day, I wanted kings, which were a bit more of a problem in the snag-filled Salmon River. While fishing for a slam one year on the Togiak, guide Bernie Ortman guided me down some of the deepest holes in the river. Precision casting and drifting red Spin-N-Glos and longlining plugs were the tickets to aggravating these husky salmon into striking. I had planned to fish the shallower chutes for silvers later that afternoon, where a good run had just started to come through, but the fishing for kings was so good I couldn't break away. The fish were pinkish red, and full of fight. The largest weighed nearly 40 pounds.

Most Grand Slam fishing is best done from shore. Water depths vary from inches to 12 or more feet in the holes. About a third of the fishing requires long-distance casting with level-wind gear, or casting flies in ever-present wind. When at all possible, pursue your slam with a fly rod.

Most of the quality streams and rivers of southwest Alaska are not more than 30 feet wide in most places, often less. These aqueous gems are excellent for sight casting flies to pink, silver and chum salmon. Watching a salmon suddenly dart out from the

One of the highlights of pursuing a Grand Slam in southwest Alaska is the spectacular scenery available throughout the region. Anglers seldom fish the same area twice in a seven-day period.

Opposite page: Silver salmon are the most aggressive of the Pacific salmon, and are easily caught on a variety of flies and lures. This silver was caught from a slough in the Mulchatna drainage.

school to engulf a fly is excitement without equal, especially when it spends more time above water than in the water! After 30 to 40 salmon strikes, per day, you are ready to retire to the tent or lodge for a relaxing drink. And that's just one species! Multiply the action times five, and you have an idea of what's in store for you. In one week I qualified for a Grand Slam three times, and still had time to fish for grayling, rainbow and char.

After the first of September, the chances of making a Grand Slam catch rapidly taper off. The last of the pinks and kings quickly disappear, with the chums taking a bit longer to die. There always seem to be sockeyes intermingled with some smaller, first-run silvers. However, the big cohos, 18-pounds and better, start entering the streams en masse toward mid September, along with seemingly countless schools of Dolly Varden.

Grand Slam salmon opportunities are not the only highlights of a visit to Alaska during "slam" time. Grayling, arctic char and rainbow fishing is spectacular in some of the remote fly-in streams. Also, ptarmigan season opens on the peninsula on August 10, and September 1 is the opener for waterfowl. A morning of bird or waterfowl hunting, followed by an afternoon of salmon fishing, is a combo that is hard to beat, anywhere in the world. Later that day, return to a shower or hot tub awaiting you at the lodge, enjoy a full-course meal, and perhaps indulge in a little after-dinner fishing.

Alaska's Grand Slam salmon fishing is more than just the taking of fish. It's wilderness, challenge and adventure all wrapped up in an experience you'll cherish for a lifetime. Yet, the magnitude of your accomplishments don't really sink in until you board the plane for the flight home. But like many of us who favor this region, chances are you'll be back. Heck, I caught my first "slam" years ago and never did leave!

Planning Your Trip

WHEN TO GO

The third and fourth week in August is the best time to pursue a Grand Slam on salmon in the Bristol Bay and Alaska Peninsula areas. This same time frame holds true for a possible slam in the Mulchatna region.

HOW TO GET THERE

Take a commercial flight to Anchorage, with a connecting flight to King Salmon or Dillingham. There, someone from one of the lodges or air taxi operations will meet you for the flight out. Some anglers arrive in Anchorage a day early to purchase any necessary flies, licenses or equipment they might need.

WHAT TO TAKE

When fishing wilderness areas, remember that there are no tackle stores around for miles. You need to be self sufficient.

A Grand Slam fishing trip requires a specialized satchel of equipment. If you're a spin/level-wind angler, take a medium-action, 6 to 7 1/2-foot spinning rod with reel filled with 12-pound mono, a medium-heavy, 7 1/2-foot level-wind rod and reel filled with 20-pound mono, and a five-foot ultralight and matching reel filled with four or 6-pound line for char, Dolly Varden, grayling and rainbow that are also present in healthy numbers. Pack a rod, matching reel and tackle in each of several duffel bags needed for your trip north. In case one gets lost or stolen, you won't be out of business. One-piece rod cases made of indestructible PVC pipe are OK, but are nearly impossible to pack on fly-out trips in the bush. Rods get banged around in planes, and broken in doors.

Fly-rodders should take a 10-weight rod for the big kings and silvers, and for casting large salmon flies in the often-present wind. A 7-weight will work nicely on the smaller salmon. Ten-foot sink tips are important, as are floating fly lines for shallow-water areas. Full-sink lines are a must for some of the deeper rivers in the area. Ensure each reel has plenty of backing. I prefer an Alvey saltwater fly reel for the 10-weight, and a Scientific Anglers System reel for the lighter rods. An anti-reverse is a must for the larger salmon.

Flies should be size 2 or 4 long and short shank, both weighted and unweighted. Conservative patterns such as spruce, boss and woolly worms are good in low, clear water, while gaudy types such as flash, Max Canyon, pink sparkler, orange roe crystal bullet, Alaska Perry fly, Baker buster and Sheary's deliverer do best in murky water.

Lures should include 1/2 to 1-ounce spoons. Go with the short, squatty types over the elongated models. Gibbs Koho, Pixee, and Kit-i-Mat in fluorescent colors work best for most anglers. Spinners with fluorescent

On some watersheds on the Alaska Peninsula, it's possible to catch all five species of Pacific salmon in one day. Anglers need to have tackle, flies and leaders prepared in advance, and spend the entire 12 hours on the water.

blades will do the job. Pack plenty in the size 3 to 5 range, and include both willow leaf and Aglia types.

Wilderness waters are cold, making neoprene waders most welcome. Take hip boots for that occasional long hike to upper headwater fishing. Polarized sunglasses are also important, as is a good hook hone and rain-gear. An extra supply of hooks, swivels, pliers, sun screen and mosquito repellent are musts. Always take an extra spool of line for each two days of fishing, and complete spools of tippet material.

HOW TO GET THERE

Charter a commercial air taxi service out of King Salmon or Dill-ingham. Several lodges offer package deals for three or more days, which includes transportation to and from the fishing areas.

WHERE TO STAY

Numerous lodges provide quality accommodations for all budgets. Full-service lodges are the most expensive, followed by established tent camp/river floats. Packing your own tent and camping gear is the least expensive.

APPROXIMATE COSTS

A typical full-service lodge charges from $2900 to $4000 for seven days of fishing. Do-it-yourself trips out of King Salmon run about $800 per person, two-person minimum.

WHO TO CONTACT

For a listing of guides, outfitters and do-it-yourself services, turn to page 208, "Free Information to Plan Your Trip."

16 *Adventure*

Most king salmon catches south of the Deep Creek Wayside take place within 200 yards of shore.

Cook Inlet's King of Kings

IT WAS 5 A.M., and I was contemplating the age-old question as to why intelligent men rise at such an ungodly hour. My coffee had turned cold, and a heavy ocean mist had turned my doughnut into a soggy lump. Daybreak was a promise yet to be fulfilled. On the horizon, a thick clump of birch trees, dark and foreboding, appeared as a pin cushion, holding long, iridescent needles of sunlight in place for what seemed to be hours.

Finally, in a radiant explosion, the pins metamorphosed into a wide-sweeping aura of light, illuminating the mile-long cliffs of Alaska's Deep Creek Marine Wayside. Fiddlehead ferns—resurrected to life from the life-inhibiting cold of an Alaska winter—continued to push their leafy heads out of isolated clumps of snow. Farther down, the beach wore a necklace of driftwood and coal chunks, laced together with 50-foot strands of kelp.

I gazed back down into the greenish water and breathed in deeply the ocean breeze. It smelled like spring; I could even taste it. But it just didn't feel like spring. Then unexpectedly, on a slight crosswind, it arrived; not with a loud bang, but with a slight tap, tap. I tensed to meet its arrival.

Before I could ease the rod out, the tip slammed down, and the

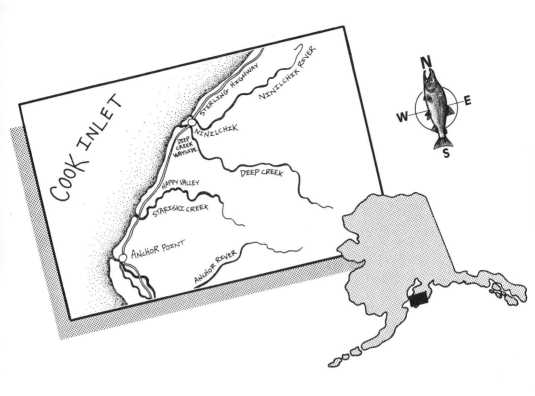

reel drag whirred away, an accolade that seemed appropriate for the occasion. Indeed, in Alaska's Cook Inlet, spring doesn't officially arrive until the springers, or first king salmon, show up along the shores of Deep Creek. And I was into one heckuva fish.

"Fish ON!" I shouted. "Fire up that motor. I'm losing line, fast!"

"Thumb down!" my friend Mike Ticconi shot back. "That fish is going to China if we don't catch him soon. Hang on."

This was a springer worth writing home about. It zigged out past the bow, then zagged back toward the stern. With torpedo-like speed, the fish suddenly sliced cross current, then out to open ocean, scorching my thumb in the process.

Mike's skillful handling of the outboard helped us gain lost line. The fish became crazed. It spiraled to the surface, threw a head-shaking, tail-slapping temper tantrum, then sizzled back into the depths. For a short while, the fish muscled the boat into the tide...stern first. However, the move proved to be the salmon's downfall. A minute later, Mike eased the net around the 52-pound, chrome-bright male. Its beefy girth and stocky tail were chromed with hundreds of minute scales, glistening in the morning sun. He had a pronounced beak or kype, as hooked as that of a parrot's. His saucer-plate-sized gills moved slowly and rhythmically, like bellows feeding the fire of life that burned within him.

167

Saltwater king salmon fishing in Cook Inlet has become the preferred method of fishing for anglers who want excitement, scenery and fish strong with power from years on the open ocean.

I removed the hook and eased the net back into the foam-flecked water. After three powerful tail flips, the salmon was gone. I slumped back in my chair, and watched on as Mike's jigging resulted in a hook-up. Indeed, spring had officially arrived in Cook Inlet.

Alaska's Cook Inlet offers what is perhaps the best saltwater king fishing in North America, if not the world. Not only is the inlet home to the largest kings found anywhere, but also some of the strongest. Cook Inlet kings are mostly wild fish, hatching from a bed of pea gravel in the semi-wilderness watersheds that feed the inlet. They'll spend anywhere from four to six years in the Gulf of Alaska—which is perhaps the richest feeding grounds in the world—putting on weight and preparing for their migratory run.

There are two runs of king salmon that migrate through Cook Inlet. The first starts showing up about mid May, peaking the third week in June. This consists of fish from 20 to 40 pounds, with an occasional fish over 60 pounds. Many of these fish are destined for Susitna and Kenai River tributary streams.

In late June or the first week in July, the second run starts. These are fish from 50 to 90 pounds, and are fewer in number than the first run. These second-run fish are considered the largest king salmon in the world, and head straight for the Kenai River.

On the average, anglers harvest 2,100 kings during the early run, and about 1,000 kings during the late run. These numbers may not sound like world-class figures, but they're darn good, especially if you consider that tens of thousands of anglers fish the streams and rivers of the Kenai Peninsula. On some Kenai Peninsula streams, anglers sometimes have to muscle each other out of the way to catch fish.

Carrie Harnisch with a respectable king salmon she caught while paddling an ocean klepper with her father, forester Fred Harnisch. Anglers can enjoy good king fishing from small boats, provided weather and tides are closely monitored.

Yet, relatively few anglers pursue these kings in their saltwater environment. Alaska Department of Fish and Game sportfish biologists say that although the fishery is growing, it is never expected to become as crowded as the Kenai River fishery. There are several reasons for this.

Cook Inlet is home to the second highest tides in the Northern Hemisphere. They can run as high as 30 feet, and can oftentimes be extremely strong. The wind percolating up from the Gulf of Alaska is always a factor. Rarely is the sea millpond smooth. I've waited for three days once for wind and wave to die down before I could launch my boat through the surf!

Boat launch facilities are fair, although crowded on the weekends. Enterprising anglers have adapted by launching from the sand and gravel beach. The favorite rig seems to be a 14 to 16-foot inflatable with a 25 to 40-horsepower motor. Cartoppers work well when the seas are calm to moderate. Those with larger boats either use the concrete ramp at the mouth of Deep Creek, or 4WDs to trailer their boats in and out of the water.

David Coray has fished Cook Inlet salmon for several years, and thinks it's one of the finest fisheries in North America. He found it so enthralling that he built a lodge on the west side of Cook Inlet.

"Cook Inlet king fishing is totally unlike the deepwater king fisheries of British Columbia and Washington," he said. "You don't need large boats for this fishery. Most of the fish migrate within 75 yards of shore, and in 12 to 25 feet of water."

Because the salmon are on a spawning migration, the salmon hug the inlet's hard clay, gravel and mud bottom, especially on an outgoing tide. On an incoming tide, fish can be found at any depth, and up to 1/4 mile from shore. The best catches occur on an incoming tide, in early morning or late evening.

On a clear day in late May, the beach at the Deep Creek Marine Wayside offers anglers a spectacular backdrop of the mountains of the Alaska and Aleutian Ranges, as well as exciting king salmon action and the makings for several fine barbecues.

Opposite page: Paul Pearson with a 64-pound king that qualified for an IGFA line-class record. He hooked the fish on a No. 7 Skagit spinner with fluorescent red hootchie skirt trailer.

However, to enjoy the best fishing, timing is critical. The peak of the run lasts only for a few days, usually around May 23 through 28. Thousands of fish, heading for the Susitna Drainage, pass through and create for exciting fishing action. I remember one year where friend Mike Ticconi and I caught and released 71 kings from 15 to 55 pounds in five days of fishing that started on May 23.

After the peak run, action remains good, but starts to taper off slowly as the fish move up the inlet.

Because Cook Inlet water is relatively shallow, and many of the kings concentrate within a narrow ribbon of water, fancy gear—such as downriggers, trolling boards and sonar gear—are not required. All you need is a rod and reel and bait or lures. One of the simplest and most effective baits to use is a rigged herring.

While it's economical to rig your own herring, several bait-holder rigs on the market make the task much simpler and faster. Choose one that allows the bait to work in a wide, slow spiral. About two to three revolutions every 36 inches is best. Run a 36 to 40 inch, 20-pound-test mono leader from the rig to a 1-to 3-ounce keel sinker; use the lighter weight for trolling closer to shore, and the larger for deepwater fish on an outgoing tide. Slowly troll the bait from 30 to 50 yards behind the boat while zig-zagging a parallel pattern to the beach.

I like to twitch the rod sharply forward every 15 seconds. This imparts a fluttering, darting movement to the already rotating herring. My experimentations have shown this action is a major factor in triggering kings to strike. Expect the take when the herring is fluttering back.

170

Lodge owner Mike McBride lifts a trap filled with Dungeness crab, a regular treat at many lodges in the Cook Inlet region. Small crabs are also a favorite food item of halibut.

If you're an artificial lure aficionado, concentrate on three basic types: large No. 7 Colorado-bladed spinners in silver/fluorescent red; one-ounce spoons in fluorescent colors, and Mepps Giant Killers. Because of the extra weight of the lures, use a smaller trolling lead. About 1 1/2 to 2 ounces is sufficient.

Here's a tip: wait until a slack tide, and troll a large, one to two ounce spoon with no weight at all. Twitch the lure as you troll shoreline structure at the slowest, possible speed. The fluttering of the spoon will allow a king to home in on it much easier, and often results in a savage strike. If the water is somewhat turbid, which is often the case after a heavy rainstorm, add a strip of prism tape for greater reflection and fish-catchability.

On either side of the inlet, you'll find fish concentrated along the freshwater/saltwater breakline, usually 15 to 200 yards down-current from where the stream or river is emptying into the inlet. Even if it isn't their natal stream, salmon will concentrate near this type of structure for several minutes or several days. Twin Falls, located several miles down the beach from Deep Creek, is a popular hangout for big kings. In other areas look for excess ground water run-off draining into the inlet. It's illegal to fish within a mile of select freshwater streams, so be sure to check the regs first.

So if you've been contemplating a fishing trip for trophy Alaska king salmon, give Cook Inlet's kings a try. I can't think of a better way to welcome the spring of the year.

Planning Your Trip

WHEN TO GO
Plan on fishing during the third week in May for numbers of fish, and the first week in July for large fish, although fewer in number.

WHAT TO TAKE
Other than the gear mentioned in the body text, take three changes of warm clothes, raingear, hip boots, poly-fill coat with hood, long underwear, stocking cap, wool socks, casual shoes. Tackle consists of a 7 1/2-foot medium-action graphite or composite rod with a limber tip yet stiff backbone. Match it with a level-wind reel in the 7000 class filled with at least 200 yards of 20-pound-test monofilament. Always bring extra line and lures.

HOW TO GET THERE
Anglers traveling to Alaska can reach Cook Inlet's Deep Creek fishery by taking commercial airlines to Anchorage, and a commuter flight directly to Kenai. Most guided operators will pick you up in Kenai. Or, reach the fishery by taking Alaska Highway 1 south, and turn off at the Deep Creek Wayside, located on the right side of the road. Recently, the Homer Spit has offered good king fishing as a result of planted stocks. Fishing is done from boat or shore.

WHERE TO STAY
During late May, accommodations are scarce. Although very crowded on weekends, one place to camp is at the Deep Creek Wayside. Lodges are available nearby. Many anglers spend the evening at hotels in Soldotna or Homer. If you want to get away from the crowds, consider flying to the west side of Cook Inlet. The area consists of semi-wilderness and wilderness areas, with a few sportfishing lodges catering to marine king salmon anglers.

APPROXIMATE COSTS
Charters run approximately $85 to $125 per person for a five-hour fishing day. Times vary, depending on tide schedules. Usually, you'll fish a few hours before high tide and two hours after. Lodges run about $250 per day and up.

WHO TO CONTACT
For a listing of guides, outfitters and do-it-yourself services, turn to page 208, "Free Information To Plan Your Trip."

17 Adventure

Pilot Dale Anderson takes a break to admire the view of an intertidal glacier in Glacier Bay National Park, located a short flight north of Admiralty Island.

Admiralty Island: Gateway to Angling Adventure

EACH YEAR, TENS OF THOUSANDS of people on their way to Alaska miss it. People looking for the "commercial" Alaska won't find it either. Even the residents of Alaska's capital city, Juneau, are often ambivalent to its unlimited outdoor opportunities. But those who have a craving to experience some of Alaska's best trout and salmon fishing, adventuring and scenic wonders recognize the portal to adventure known as Admiralty Island.

Trying to appreciate the potential of Admiralty Island from Juneau or anywhere else is much like looking through an opaque glass: something is there, but the details are fuzzy and obscure. But a 10-minute flight from Juneau International Airport to the heart of Admiralty Island will make it clear as to why this island was designated as a National Monument by presidential proclamation in 1978.

Emerald-green coastal forests stretch down to secluded bays colored by the sapphire-blue sea. Deer graze in both alpine pastures and on sandy, shell-covered beaches. Whales shatter the quiet surface as they breach off distant points, and the sweet taste of

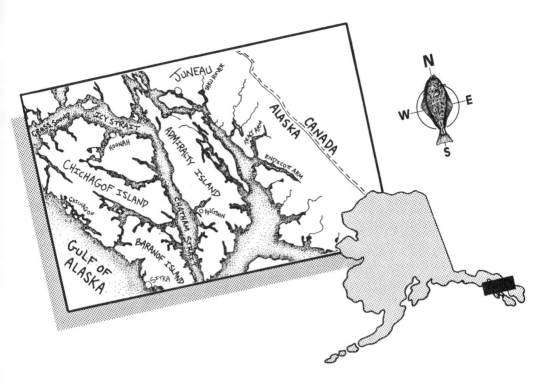

spring water and succulent huckleberries are the "milk and honey" that await the visitor. Indeed, it doesn't take long to appreciate the wonders of Admiralty and her surrounding beauty.

Pilot Dale Anderson was eager to introduce me to Admiralty when he met me with float-plane ready upon my arrival at Juneau International. The introduction didn't take long. Within minutes we were on a day-long flightseeing tour over the island and nearby mainland glaciers. We circled mountain goats perched atop precipitous peaks, watched whales porpoise, their huge size making their actions seem like slow motion. But the spectacle—the area that kept me spell-bound in my seat for what seemed to be hours was Glacier Bay National Park.

Unlike parks in the Lower 48, this area is a 4,400-square-mile wilderness with a restricted road system. Therefore, most of the sightseeing is done by air or boat. But flightseeing Glacier Bay with Anderson was nothing less than spectacular. The Fairweather Range of the St. Elias Mountains, and the 16 tidewater glaciers in this area, are awe-inspiring. As we flew over one, a 200-foot berg broke off and crashed into the bay.

In contrast, the experience was humbling also. As Dale pulled on the flaps, we circled over a "river of mud" that shot from a hole in the side of a tidewater glacier. The geological forces at work were incredible. Later, in a nearby bay, we saw thousands of seals stretch out on massive ice chunks beneath the face of a glacier. They

When fishing Admiralty Island, think bears! Biologists estimate one brown bear for every square mile, the highest concentration in North America.

Opposite page: Streams and lakes on Admiralty offer a bounty of wild foods such as freshwater clams, blueberries and cutthroat trout.

strained to lift their brownish heads, only to plop them down on the ice and resume sleeping. After all, we were no threat to them.

At lunchtime, Dale settled at the head of a remote bay and taxied up to the face of a towering tidewater glacier. The greenish-blue water—caused by the refraction of light off the microscopic particles of glacial silt—cast dancing shapes and colors onto chunks of bluish-tinged ice that drifted by.

After some exploring, we took off in order to "make a date" with a salmon tide that evening. With Juneau about a half-hour flight away, I was curious as to why we were leaving so early for a tide that was scheduled eight hours later. I soon had my answer as we flew inland.

The floats cut the glassy surface of an alpine lake. The engine coughed to a stop, and the quiet and serenity eased me into a relaxed fishing mood. Dale didn't need to tell me this was one of those isolated freshwater gems that receive little fishing pressure for cutthroat trout. Just as I thought about what to use, a cutt jumped in shallow water.

"Most of these cutts are from six to 12 inches," he said. "Of course, there are several lakes that grow cutts up to eight pounds, but this lake is noted more for numbers of fish rather than size."

He was right. Casting flies and ultralight lures around the lake, we found the cutts to be not only aggressive but constantly on the feed. The fish were not large by any means. But size is secondary in importance in such a grand environment. We had the entire lake

to ourselves. Neither plane nor person appeared on the lake nor noise interrupt our pursuit. The sun burned brightly overhead, making for short-sleeve weather. And to our surprise, there were no mosquitoes.

After four hours of catch-and-release cutt fishing, we headed back to base camp located in quiet Funter Bay. The main lodge was hand-hewn from logs and handcrafted into place by a Swedish homesteader in 1949, and the entire camp is a testimony to him and his wife's lifestyle. The current caretakers stayed busy by cooking such outstanding meals as crab and halibut, steak, and huckleberry pancakes. They also kept the kayaks, fishing gear and sleeping rooms in immaculate condition.

After dinner, Dale and his brother Greg, told me a bit about the fishing potential at Admiralty.

"We have a variety of species, which include all five species of salmon, halibut, ling cod, rockfish, Dolly Varden, steelhead and cutthroat and rainbow trout in several of the alpine lakes," Greg said. "Most of the fishing is done from a boat or by casting from shore, which keeps you busy." He said that world-renown wildlife artist Robert Bateman and his family recently visited Admiralty Island for several days and they caught 13 silver salmon, two halibut weighing over 30 pounds, and plenty of rockfish on light tackle.

"They really enjoyed pulling the Dungeness crab pots," Dale said.

The author casting for pink and chum salmon in Donkey Bay, located on the southern end of Admiralty Island. During early August, the saltwater is often black with in-migrating salmon.

"I think they caught 23 the first day. Bateman liked the salmon also. He took his catch home to feed to royalty that were to visit him in a few weeks."

With the fishing, scenic beauty and wildlife, Dale said the family loved the area. He quoted Bateman as saying, "My family has never had a treasure like this," in reference to Admiralty Island.

I could see the truth in that comment after we pulled up to the pink salmon stream. The fish were congregated in an intertidal area at the stream's mouth, where they would eventually spawn.

"Looks like a large number of fish are here," Dale said, pointing to one, then another, and still yet another pink as it porpoised in on the high tide.

However, I soon discovered that "large number of fish" was an understatement. There were so many fish in the area that each time they moved, a foot-high tidal wave would quickly break our way. Salmon continually bumped into our legs as we waded out onto the shallow gravel bar. At times, the wave of fish was so unexpected that we jokingly ran for the safety of the boat.

In its final contribution of the day, the setting sun created an orange aura of light that silhouetted Dale and Greg, along with hundreds of porpoising pink salmon. After two hours of nearly a fish a cast, it didn't take long to burn out on catching fish. We weren't tired of fishing, it's just that our arms couldn't take any more of the abuse ocean-strong pinks had been dishing out on our ultralight tackle.

Silver salmon are abundant in the intertidal areas of Admiralty. Pybus Bay and Admiralty Cove are good locations for anglers wishing to spin or fly cast for in-migrating salmon.

But I soon discovered there were other fishers nearby, also. On an ancient piling, a fish crow screamed its guttural territorial call at a black spruce. A closer look rewarded me with the full image of a bald eagle, watching the spawning activity of the salmon with seeming disinterest. Suddenly, out of nowhere, a gull dropped into a kamikaze dive to within inches of the eagle before pulling up and screaming a series of admonitions at it.

"The eagles swoop down on the gulls and their young during nesting season," Dale explained. "You can say there's a bit of animosity between the two species."

After a late return to my cabin, the last thing I expected was an "alarm clock" waking me up at 5 a.m. Like everything else at Funter Bay, at least the screams of Steller jays outside were natural. Yet it's a scolding, raspy noise that grates the silence of the forest. However, the birds soon allow the newcomer his own branch, and all resume feeding...quietly!

A quick glance out over the saltwater flats prompted a chuckle as I watched a stilt-legged blue heron stalk the shallows for crabs and baitfish. The bird is truly a master fisher, and a living example of patience in its purest form. I was engrossed in watching him stalk the shallows, watching, always watching and waiting without moving a feather. Then, almost faster than I can blink, the heron made a piercing jab to capture its prey. After the catch, he tossed his head up and swallowed the fish before again repeating the waiting sequence.

Through my spotting scope, I powered in on the heron's head. His large, yellow eyes were almost sinister looking, but full of ex-pression, especially after the bird ruffled its feathers in the misty

Glacier Bay and surrounding waters offer spectacular scenery as well as excellent fishing for halibut, salmon and rockfish.

rain. It's as if he were saying, "Boy, that feels good. But what am I doing out here in the rain? The fishing is lousy!"

Before breakfast, and while photographing the morning dew on an old vise I found in the forest, I looked up to see a blacktail doe staring directly at me. She moved off after making sure I was no threat, and began feeding on a variety of ferns and grasses. On the beach, she jumped onto an old fish trap and fed on the succulent grasses that grew between driftwood logs. I stalked to within 10 feet of her. What a challenge! However, the clicking of my camera quickly alerted her and piqued her curiosity. Hiding behind a rock, I heard the doe sneaking toward me, her head down and nose, ears and eyes trying to determine whether or not I was a threat. After tossing her head this way and that, she slowly grazed off in a non-threatened manner.

Walking along Admiralty's shoreline is refreshing for the soul. All problems, all thoughts that predominate in city living, are erased with the steps in the fine, squishy sand. Beds of mussels rise a short distance out of the rocks, their purplish sheen glimmering a cobalt blue in the afternoon sun. Shells abound, as do starfish and small crabs scurrying for the safety of a rock. It's important to experience Admiralty by yourself, preferably in the early morning, to fully appreciate the day's sights and activities: the abandoned canneries; a creek where you can photograph brown bears fishing for salmon; or fish for salmon yourself, either from shore or trolling from a boat. In this marine fishery, king salmon fight with powerful splendor, while the cohos and other salmon leap with a vigor unlike those fish found in freshwater. If you want your fishing trip to Alaska to not only be remembered for catching fish, but also for the interaction between Nature and the land, then take notice of Admiralty Island. You'll be glad you did.

Planning Your Trip

WHEN TO GO

July is the best month for pink, chum, sockeye and king salmon. Saltwater silver salmon fishing is best in mid August, and in freshwater, September. Dolly Varden fishing is best in July and August, and again in October. April, May and October are the best months for steelheading, and May and June for cutthroat trout, although lake resident fish can be caught all summer long.

WHAT TO TAKE

If staying in any of the U.S. Forest Service cabins, take food, sleeping bag and pad, cooking stove and utensils, outboard motor. Quality raingear is a must, as well as ankle-fit hip boots, especially when hiking the Admiralty Lakes Recreation Area. A 6-weight flyrod is a good, all-around rod for Admiralty; consider an 8-weight for chums and silvers. My favorite flies include chartreuse sparkle shrimp, Glo-Bugs, muddler minnows and leech flies. For trout in lakes, stonefly and scud patterns work exceptionally well.

HOW TO GET THERE

From Anchorage or Seattle, take Alaska Airlines to Juneau, and charter a plane or boat to Admiralty Island, located directly across Stephens Passage, a flight of several minutes. Various parts of Admiralty Island are accessible by boat and trail. The Admiralty Lakes Recreation Area Canoe Trail offers excellent fishing for cutthroat, Dollies, landlocked salmon and rainbow trout. You'll need at least a week to properly fish this trail. Boats can drop you off with canoe or kayak at the trailhead. Be sure to arrange a pick-up time.

WHERE TO STAY

U.S. Forest Service cabins offer inexpensive, overnight accommodations. Several lodges, as well as charter boats, provide either permanent or mobile bases from which to tour and fish the island. Take along a backpack and tent for an occasional overnight spike camp when hiking in to various fishing locales. Use caution, however, as bears are numerous.

WHAT TO DO

On or based from Admiralty Island, you can enjoy any or all these possibilities for an Alaska adventure of a lifetime: glacier flightseeing; cutthroat, halibut, rockfish, salmon (pink, king, silver, chum) and Dolly Varden fishing; participate in the Golden North Salmon Derby; scuba diving; wildlife viewing for goat, deer, eagle, and bear; saltwater and freshwater kayaking; explore isolated coves; alpine camping; berry picking and crabbing.

APPROXIMATE COSTS

Do-it-yourselfers can enjoy a bare-bones trip on Admiralty for the major cost of reaching the various trailheads, which can range from free (get there yourself by boat) to $800 or more, round trip for a fly-in to the southern, western half of the island. Lodges and motor yachts charge about $3,000 for a week's fishing/adventure tour of the area.

WHO TO CONTACT

For a listing of guides, outfitters and do-it-yourself services, turn to page 208, "Free Information To Plan Your Trip."

18 *Adventure*

A Dolly Varden char in full spawning colors taken in mid August from the Sagavanirktok River, Arctic National Wildlife Refuge.

Fishing Alaska's Last Great Wilderness—The Arctic National Wildlife Refuge

OF ALL THE AREAS TO FISH IN ALASKA, the Arctic National Wildlife Refuge (ANWR), located in the far, northeast corner of the state, is perhaps the most coveted of all wildlife refuges in Alaska. No, it doesn't have huge runs of salmon or an unlimited supply of trophy-class fish. It has something far greater. It has the charm, elegance and grace of being the aristocrat of all wilderness fishing areas.

When you first look at her, you know, deep within, this is the place you have always dreamed of fishing: unspoiled mountains, plains free of settlements and cities, and few boats or people crowding the river. Aircraft traffic is minimal at all hours of the day. Without the man-made noise pollution, you can hear birds singing, ducks dabbling across the lake's surface, or glacially scarred rocks tumbling down an avalanche chute. These are Nature's musicians in the act of creating a one-of-a-kind wilderness concerto for you alone to hear.

But ANWR might not always offer these bonuses, especially if

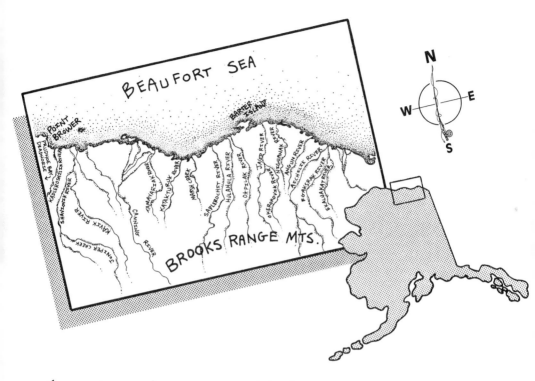

the area is opened up to massive oil development within the next few years. Luckily, there is still time for you to experience this refuge as it exists now.

ANWR is not a mega-sportfishery like Bristol Bay, but it is noteworthy in its own right. The Beaufort Sea is one of the richest marine environments in the world. The sea is home to fat, anadromous char and whitefish. In freshwater areas, sportsmen seek equally husky arctic grayling, lake trout and burbot. Pink and chum salmon are also available, along with a variety of ciscoes.

However, the char is the most popular sportfish species found throughout the region, in intertidal as well as freshwater systems. There are two forms of char in ANWR: an eastern lake dweller located in the Canning River drainage, and the western form which is distributed throughout the river, streams and lakes of the area.

It's safe to say that the Canning River offers the best char fishing in ANWR. All four types; non-anadromous lake residents, non-anadromous spring residents; non-anadromous stream dwellers known as "residual" char, and anadromous stream dwellers are all found there. Residual populations are found throughout the Canning, Hulahula and Aichilik systems; lake resident char are plentiful in the lakes of the Jago River, Peters and Schrader lakes, and the lower portion of the Canning River drainage.

183

The Canning, Hulahula, Aichilik, Egaksrak and Kongakut rivers all contain anadromous populations of arctic char, any of which could offer a spectacular fishing adventure.

Here's a tip: these anadromous char move freely along the entire coastline of ANWR, and are caught in major lagoons. Studies show the char prefer the nearshore brackish waters over the open marine waters, a plus if you're visiting Prudhoe Bay. Take your rod and make a few casts off the jetties or into the bays in the area. Also expect good concentrations of char on the seaward side of the Barrier Islands. Action here is often a fish per cast.

Anadromous char migrate into the intertidal areas at break-up, and move back into streams as early as late June. Peak movement into the Canning River occurs from late July through August, perhaps the most spectacular time to fish this area. Bugs are not as ferocious in late June, plus the fall colors are gorgeous.

What's so amazing about these fish is not their size, but their age. The severe winter climate is responsible for slow growth in some populations of fish. A resident char taken at Big Lake, located at the headwaters of the Canning River, was 16 years old and only 6.4 inches long. Of course, the anadromous char are much larger. The fastest growing and largest are found in the Kongakut River. Fish of 27.5 to 33 inches have been taken by biologists from this watershed. They run 8 to 10 pounds, are excellent fighting fish, and handsomely colored. However, the Kongakut receives some fishing pressure.

ANWR char are opportunistic feeders. In the lagoons, they feed on crustaceans and fish. Non-anadromous stream residents depend primarily on midges, and stonefly and mayfly nymphs.

Opposite page: When flying to or from ANWR, be sure to stop and visit the Arrigetch Peaks, located in the Gates of the Arctic National Park. Although a bit out of the way, the scenery is well worth your time. And the fishing is excellent in nearby lakes and rivers.

At left: When walking along streams and lakes in the arctic, anglers should keep an eye open for gems, agates and quartz crystals, like this one dwarfing this Minolta 35mm camera.

Adult spawners apparently cease feeding when they enter the freshwater streams to spawn. However, they do strike lures as well as attractor and forage fish-imitating flies, such as sand lance, smolt, herring, and shiner patterns in sizes 1/0 to 4.

I remember my first fishing trip to the Canning for char. We were flown in and dropped off on a gravel bar for a short float trip. Once the plane disappeared in the distance, megadoses of quiet permeated the environment.

The Canning was made to be a fly fishing stream. I walked the ridges above the meandering water, looking for pools or runs that held husky grayling and char. I found it challenging to stalk within casting distance of a fish-holding pool without benefit of brush or trees. There were no prying eyes, no fishing pressure, no guides to impress. Only endless miles of barren tundra. I enjoyed the simple act of fly fishing; listening to the swishing of my fly line through guides, executing upstream mends, and false casting, just for the heck of it, watching my line stretch out over a panorama of arctic wilderness.

The polar shrimp sank quickly, and the ensuing strike was full of aggression, as if the fly was the tastiest morsel found in arctic waters. The fish was a typical char: it rolled incessantly and bulldogged for bottom, followed by lots of splashing in the shallows.

ANWR offers vast expanses of tundra that is home to the Central Arctic and Porcupine caribou herds, two of the state's largest. In the spring, thousands of caribou can be found near the Canning River, giving birth to calves. Anglers will find caribou sign abundant in ANWR.

The fish was a vivid green and orange, complemented by pinkish-red circles adorning its flanks. After removing the fly, I eased the fish into the current and absorbed the pure ecstasy of the moment. It's a feeling that still gives me butterflies to this day.

Walking down the bank, I noticed that ANWR sights are small and easily overlooked. Arctic avens, which grow profusely, color the greenish carpet on the terraces above the river, which offer the best vantage point to look for holding areas. American dippers, small birds which dive for their food, flutter along the riverbank. An occasional diving duck would skitter across the surface. These sights were just a handful of many that complemented the fishing for char and grayling, which was the best this country had to offer.

In Shainin Lake, arctic char average 20.7 inches at 11 years of age. The lake, located at 2,756 feet elevation, is approximately 1,400 surface acres. Fish feed on snails, mollusks and chironomids taken from the lake bottom. Due to glacial run-off, the water is a milky blue when seen from the air. The best fishing for char and lakers is at the inlets and outlets of the lake. Fishing is slow in mid lake. For best success, work your flies and lures in 20 to 40 feet of water.

Kurupa Lake lies in a mountainous bowl at 3,020 feet elevation, and is 16 miles west of the Killik River Valley. The lake has 100 surface acres, two inlets and one outlet. Known depths range from 32 to 50 feet. The shores on the west and east sides are algae covered, while the outlet is strewn with large boulders. Water temperature is suited for lakers and char, running in the upper 40s and low 50s. This is a top choice for a get-away fishing trip, or as a base of operations for further exploration in the area. Kurupa Lake fish run 17 inches at 11 years of age.

Grayling in the Arctic National Wildlife Refuge are extremely slow-growing fish. Biological surveys indicate that a 17-inch fish can be 20 years old.

Lake trout are found in the Colville River and numerous other lakes deep enough to support them, such as the Teshekpuk, east of ANWR, Okpilak Lake, and Peters and Schrader lakes. According to biologists, lakers up to 35 inches and 14 pounds are taken from the latter two lakes. Stomach analyses indicate that only half of all lake trout sampled had food in their stomachs, consisting of least cisco, snails, aerial insects, round whitefish, slimy sculpin, and voles. Of 11 lake trout stomachs examined, researchers found grayling in two fish, decomposed fish remains in six fish, plant debris in one fish, and two fish with empty stomachs.

Jigging lures from one-half to six ounces are especially effective here, with gold, silver, olive drab and blue-white the most effective colors. On cloudy days, chartreuse was particularly effective, either in flies or plugs. Gold Wiggle Warts work exceptionally well when trolled as slow as possible along lake shore structure.

An exceptionally good lake for large lakers is Shainin Lake. Fish average 21 inches, and can reach 30 inches. Other lakes? At Tulugak Lake, average length is 19 inches for 12-year-old fish; Chandler Lake, 22 inches for 14-year-old fish; Kurupa Lake, 23 inches, 18-year-old fish; and Itkillik Lake, 16 inches, 11 years old. A note here on the Itkillik: this is a moderately high and scenic mountain lake in the Colville drainage. Surface area is 1,330 acres, with a maximum reported depth of up to 41 feet. A single outlet can be found on the south end, and several small inlet streams are on the eastern hillside, which provide good fishing. In addition to lake trout, whitefish and grayling are present in good numbers at these inlets, and in the outlet, especially after ice-out.

Grayling are the most widely distributed fish in ANWR. Fish up to 19 inches are taken from the Canning River in July and August.

Some of the best fishing in ANWR takes place in late summer on the Kongakut, Hulahula and Canning rivers. Snow comes early, so most trips should be planned before early September.

However, most average from 13 to 15 inches. Grayling, too, get very old in the ANWR area. In test nettings, the oldest fish caught was a 20-year-old male, 17.3 inches long, taken from the Tamayariak River. Grayling captured by hook and line in the Sadlerochit River, and its main tributary the Itkilyariak River, were in the 12-to 15-inch range.

Food items of ANWR grayling include caddis fly larvae, chironomids and small forage fish. However, most any natural looking pattern will catch fish.

Small runs of pink and chum salmon occur in the Colville and Mackenzie rivers. Occasionally, salmon are caught from the Canning and Sagavanirktok rivers. There is insufficient data regarding the area's salmon population. Therefore, do not plan a trip to ANWR with the sole purpose of catching salmon.

ABOUT OTHER WATERS

The Colville is a large river, spanning 600 feet wide in places, with depths averaging 16 feet to a maximum of 27 feet. It is the largest waterway draining to the north coast of Alaska. The river undergoes ice breakup from its headwaters to its mouth beginning in early May, and is navigable by mid June. While the Colville is very clear, it is subject to rapid and large rises in water levels due to rainfall. During months of light rainfall, boat travel is difficult, due to the braided nature of the river. A small outboard is necessary on the lower end.

The Itkillik River is about 175 miles long, and drains an area of approximately 2,000 square miles. The river has broad, sweeping curves with mid stream shoals about eight miles above the mouth.

Maximum water depth near the mouth is about seven to nine feet. Arctic char, grayling, lake trout and whitefish are all present in good numbers.

The Anaktuvuk River is a clear, rapid stream, about 123 miles in length. Average depth is 2.5 feet near the mouth, with pools running as deep as five feet during the summer months. The river offers excellent fishing for large grayling, and is good for arctic char, lake trout, burbot and round whitefish.

Whether or not ANWR will be explored for oil is still undecided at this time. However, it's a sure bet that if exploration begins, the wilderness fisheries in this region will incur additional fishing pressure and congestion. Many rivers, such as the Canning and those close to Prudhoe Bay, will receive increasing amounts of aircraft traffic. For a wilderness fishery, this is the kiss of death.

So don't delay. If you can appreciate the wonder of cradling in your palm a 12-year-old, 15-inch grayling, floating for days through treeless tundra, or spending the afternoon basking in the rocky framework of a glacial cirque, ANWR could very well be your ticket to one of the last great fishing adventures in North America.

Planning Your Trip

ABOUT THE AREA

For a wilderness float that doesn't receive much pressure, choose the Canning. You have your choice of a 45 to 50-mile, or a 90 to 100-mile float. The mid river is the best for fishing, and July and August is the best time for both char and grayling.

The Canning is a premier wilderness float. Expect to see Dall sheep, moose, and lots of caribou, especially near the pick-up point. In years of normal water flow, there are no large whitewater rapids on this river. Also, anglers and outdoor groups have yet to discover the full potential of floating this river.

In recent years, the Kongakut and the Hulahula have been receiving moderate pressure from backpackers and floaters, a point to consider if you're looking for wilderness isolation as much as unique fishing opportunities.

WHEN TO GO

Depending on the severity of the winter, ice out takes place in early to mid June. Fishing is good through the first of September, when snow storms and freezing temperatures begin to restrict air access. August has always been my favorite month for a float. Fall colors, as well as concentrations of spawning char and grayling, provide for optimum fishing opportunities.

WHAT TO TAKE

ANWR summers are short and cool, and generally cloudy along the coast, while remaining warm and sunny in and around the mountains. Pack Thinsulate or fiber-fill base clothing, as evenings can be chilly and the wind is usually blowing, especially in late summer. In the mountains, it can snow at any time. Neoprenes help keep you warm and dry, but if you plan on any cross-country hiking, take either hiking boots or ankle-fit hip boots.

For lake fishing, take ultralight spinning tackle and a heavier rod for deepwater trolling and/or jigging. Tiny 1/64 ounce to 1/8- ounce spoons in silver, gold and rainbow-prism work well. Also effective are 1/2-ounce weight-forward spinners, 1/4 to 1-ounce leadhead jigs in white and black, and floating plugs to be fished off a Baitwalker or Poor Man's Downrigger. (This system is used to find fish in a lake. Once fish are found, switch to fly fishing or ultralight jigging). Large flatfish in gold and mottled brown or pearl finish are also effective.

Fly fishing enthusiasts should remember that char, laker and grayling fishing is best in lakes right after ice out. Fish are cruising the outlets, islands, and other structure, feeding on mosquito larvae, chironomids, odonata nymphs as well as other aquatic insects. With the exception of grayling, the larger char and lakers seem to be caught on forage fish patterns such as stickleback, sculpin and blue smolt, shiner, and herring patterns in sizes 2 through 2/0.

In streams and rivers, size 6 through 10 marabou muddlers and leech patterns are exceptionally good, as well as hare's ear nymph and various caddisfly patterns. In fall, size 10 peach egg patterns work best.

Unless you have your own plane, an ANWR trip is one that requires just the bare basics for survival and fishing. It's always possible to ship your gear to Fort Yukon via parcel post. This will save you $50 to $100 or more on extra freight charges. When you depart, use the same shipping cartons and ship them back to your home. Be sure to ship in plenty of time, prior to your arrival in Fort Yukon, usually six to eight weeks. Ship in care of General Delivery, or insured in your name or the air charter operator's business. Inquire about water conditions before you depart on your trip. No rain can mean very low water in some areas, creating for a less than desirable float. Pilots who fly the area are familiar with conditions, and will advise you accordingly. Thus, it's always good to have a back-up or secondary plan or destination.

HOW TO GET THERE

Reaching ANWR is not difficult, although it is expensive. If you have a group of less than nine, take a commercial flight to Fairbanks, where you'll book with any of several air charter services to Fort Yukon. Another alternative is to fly commercial from Fairbanks to Arctic Village, and have a charter operator waiting there to fly you directly to the river or lake of choice.

WHERE TO STAY

To fully appreciate the beauty and wilderness environment of ANWR, I suggest a do-it-yourself float trip down one of several rivers listed, or a five-day stay on a wilderness lake. A mountaineering type tent is a prerequisite for camping in this region, as windstorms in excess of 60 m.p.h. are common. A handful of guides based in Fairbanks, Fort Yukon and Bettles offer float trips as well as fly-in fishing.

APPROXIMATE COSTS

To Fort Yukon, round-trip fare runs about $120 per person, with 40 pounds of allowable baggage. Anything in excess is charged about 40 cents a pound. Cost out of Fort Yukon aboard a Beaver is about $800 for two people and gear. Additional cost for heavy loads. Lake fishing runs in the $750 range. Several air taxi operators offer complete boat and equipment rental packages at reasonable rates.

WHO TO CONTACT

For a listing of guides, outfitters and do-it-yourself services, turn to page 208, "Free Information To Plan Your Trip."

19 Adventure

Adela Batin battles a Chuitna River king salmon as it takes off for deeper water.

The Challenging Chinooks of Alaska's Chuit River

AT FIRST GLANCE, THERE WAS NOTHING particularly special about the group of seven anglers boarding a Dehaviland Beaver on a remote lake on Alaska's Kenai Peninsula. All were adult men, doing what men do best, squirming for the best seat on the plane, providing a liberal backdrop of jokes, and questioning the pilot about the oil leak on the engine.

A closer look revealed the anglers shared a surprising number of similarities. All were clad in hip boots, held new fishing rod tubes of various sizes, and were overdressed for the 65-degree weather. There was another common bond. They had forsaken the allure of the famous Kenai River fishery—only a few miles away—and its world-class trophy kings and shoulder-to-shoulder anglers. Instead, they had each purchased the best king fishing action $185 could buy on a little-known, away from the crowds stream called the Chuitna River.

Expectations were not high. Alaska sportfish advertising hype being what it is, the anglers realized that if the group caught a couple of fish, the trip would be worthwhile. After all, they would

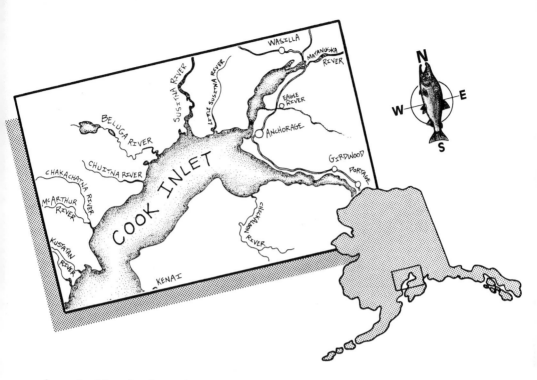

be only 30 miles from the Kenai. If anything, the trip would be relaxing.

Little did they realize that the trip would be far from relaxing. It would be more than they bargained for.

During the 20-minute flight, two visitors sat with their mouths agape as an Alaska resident told stories of Cook Inlet, with its 30-foot killer tides, quicksand-like mud flats and killer whales. Another's features were a pale green and tightlipped from the inlet's roller coaster turbulence that rocked the plane. The remainder of the party sat in quiet reflection, wondering if they had made the right decision.

After landing on the west side of Cook Inlet, the adventure continued. The visitors unloaded their gear and waited for a ride to the upper river. For nearly a half hour they bounced down a gravel trail in a van where the muffler and most of the vehicle's screws had long since vibrated out. The road dust choked them, and the mosquitoes attacked them mercilessly. As if this wasn't tribulation enough, there was the long climb down into the Chuitna riverbed. Each angler hung on to a 200-foot long rope, taking it one step at a time. One slip could mean a rolling fall of several hundred feet.

Despite these hindrances, Travis Price was the first to arrive on the Chuitna, a meandering waterway often no more than 15 feet across. He assembled a heavy-action salmon rod and reel, sat on a huge lump of coal, and waited for guide Dan Leis.

Fresh-from-the-sea Chuit kings are rough on tackle, as evidenced by this straightened swivel and extra stong siwash hook.

Having neither caught nor fished for king salmon, Price held his anxiety well. He openly talked about the friend from whom he borrowed the rod and reel he was using.

"My friend Joe has fished the Kenai River for three years," Price said. "He has a boat, fancy equipment, and has yet to catch a king. But lately, I've heard people comment that the Chuitna is the place to go for king salmon. On the way over, our pilot said that the fishing was so good, that people were canceling their trips on the Kenai to fish the Chuitna. Maybe I'll get lucky and catch one."

Price dropped the discussion and turned his attention to his tackle box. For over a minute there was nothing but the melancholy chattering of the Chuitna and the far-off conversation of guide Dan Leis coming down the trail. Then it started. The slow patter-patter of water, followed by the blast-off surge of a ocean-fresh king rocketing up through 10 inches of water. The salmon's undulating tail kicked up plumes of spray, its wide, girthy shoulders flashing and rippling with unharnessed power, signaling a dare to any and all takers. Price smiled, the corner of his mouth moving round and round, like a horse chomping at the bit.

"Forget that spoon," said Leis, grabbing a Spin-N-Glo and pencil-lead rig from a small plastic bag. With fingers the color of red chili peppers caused by the salmon-egg dye, he tied the rig onto a three-way swivel.

"Now for the ingredient that makes this rig irresistible to salmon." From a Zip-loc bag Leis pulled a cube of salmon roe dyed fluorescent red. As he squeezed the roe into the egg loop, the dye

Guide Dan Leis, right, hoists a king for his client. The Chuit is a three to four-day king fishery. Many anglers, however, get burned out on catching fish the first day.

oozed out onto his fingers. He wiped the goo onto his jacket.

"You're set, partner," he said to Price. "Stand right there and cast into that pool. Drift the rig down that far channel, right along bottom. That's where the salmon are."

Price's rig never reached bottom. A silvery king saw the fluorescent glob and grabbed it. Fish and angler—both newcomers to this freshwater environment—entered a state of limbo for a second, a measure of time that often lasts for an eternity for those watching the tell-tale signs of a solid take. Finally, Price's hookset triggered an explosion of excitement. Twice the fish took to the air, shaking and thrashing its dime-bright flanks. The fiberglass rod cracked and moaned in protest. Catapulting into a perfect figure eight aerial, the salmon hit the water, whirled around the pool, creased the shallow edge of the gravel bar, and returned to the main channel, all in a matter of seconds.

Both fish and angler readily exchanged and absorbed power blows. In opposing corners, like managers at ringside, Leis shouted advice to his fighter, while Nature's call to survive and spawn encouraged hers. Time would be the referee.

Finally, with the pride of a manager reaching out to grab the trophy for his champ, Leis tailed the salmon, held it up for an admiring glance from Price, and pointed it back upstream. In a shower of spray that shouted spunky defiance rather than thanks, the fish shot back into the current and resumed its upstream journey. The other anglers stood mesmerized. They had yet to wet a line.

As Leis rigged the other rods, he talked about the growing

popularity of the Chuitna fishery.

"Chuitna king salmon are some of the wildest you'll find anywhere," he said. "We're only 12 miles from the inlet, and the fish we catch are fresh and feisty. Many of the fish range from 20 to 30 pounds, but there are lots of 50-pounders caught. The largest to date has been a 65-pounder."

Leis said that many do-it-yourself anglers fish the lower stretch of river. However, the best success is upstream, in the clearwater pools not affected by the tide. Also, knowing where to and how to fish for in-migrating salmon is of vital importance. It's evident that Leis and fellow guide Mitch Posey have that knowledge. On the flight over, pilot Doug Brewer said that anglers on guided trips with Leis and Posey were 100 percent successful in catching Chuitna king salmon.

During the peak of the season, the success rate can be more than 100 percent: it can be devastating. Mike Solovy of Vernon, California, spoke from first-hand experience.

"I fished with my group yesterday," he said while holding out his drift lure for Leis to rebait. "Those guys got so tuckered out from catching salmon, they're spending the day recouping at the hotel. I couldn't resist, and had to come back. I caught over 25 kings yesterday. I'm definitely coming back next year, and bringing my kid."

According to Posey, the Chuitna king fishery starts around mid June, with salmon entering the river until the second week in July. Fishing remains excellent until the last of July. And unlike other streams, the Chuitna has conditions perfect for fly fishing: low, clear water, wide gravel bars free of trees and debris, and a relatively slow current in the upper river. According to Posey, the best time for fly fishing is the first three weeks in July, after the water has had a chance to clear from spring run-off.

"We had a client land a 48-pounder late last evening on a fly," he said. "It was the thrill of his life. Then he proceeded to catch and release several others."

Later that day, Jeral Manning of Bakersville, California, grunted as he set the hook into a sleek, 30-pound-plus king. The fish surged upstream, before catching the main current and departing for parts unknown around the next bend.

"Help!" Manning cried, as he rounded a corner. "I'm losing ground!"

"Heck on you," someone replied, jokingly. "We're busy fishing."

This type of conversation was typical of Manning's group, at this point merely heady from king fishing overindulgence. By mid day, these five Californians had already caught the fish they had planned to take home. With 14-year-old entrepreneur R.J. Ripper

Travis Price examines a piece of aircraft wreckage he found embedded in the bank on the Chuit River. Low hanging clouds, violent wind gusts and soft sand, combined with pilot error, have contributed to many accidents.

charging five dollars a salmon to pack the group's fish up the 200-foot cliff, the group abandoned all sense of fish-care responsibility and indulged in catching and releasing 20 to 40-pound kings.

It was obvious that salmon fishing insanity, a common epidemic in these parts, had taken root. By the time the fish towed Manning back upstream, he faced a medley of shouting, whooping and hollering as two of his friends battled kings. The two remaining anglers without fish drew fillet knives and pretended to cut the lines of those who did.

Manning, after releasing his king, sat on a nearby log for a breather.

"I regularly fish for marlin and other saltwater species out of Cabo San Lucas, and this is the best fishing I've ever experienced. The atmosphere is so totally different. I'm coming back."

Mike Hatch of Bakersfield, California, was impressed not only with the king fishing, but some halibut fishing his group had experienced the day before on Cook Inlet.

"This Chuitna River and Cook Inlet are fantastic," he said, taking a bite out of a two-inch thick sandwich. "Yesterday, our party chartered a boat out of Homer. We caught and released a half-dozen 40-pound halibut just 70 miles south of here. I kept a 100-pounder for the barbecue. The others kept their limit of two fish each, which together totaled more than 500 pounds of fillets."

After the Californians had left for the day, Travis Price slowly walked the banks of the Chuitna. There was more here to discover

An aerial view of the lower Chuit River, where it empties into Cook Inlet. Heavy brush and bears discourage anglers from brush busting any distance up river.

than just salmon. Brown bear tracks were pressed deep and wide into the white sand, dwarfing the size 11 hip boot prints. And near a boulder-rimmed sandbar, he unearthed a piece of plane wreckage. Did the pilot stall the plane, or was he a victim of a downdraft or sudden gust of wind? Did he live, or die? Indeed, the call of Chuitna salmon is strong, and in this country, the price of mistakes can cost dearly.

The area is also a haven to an abundance of wildlife, but most impressive are the marine mammals that follow the salmon into the lower river.

"You'll see seals coming in to feed on salmon," said guide Dennis Torrey. "But it's really a sight when you see huge beluga and killer whales chasing salmon right up on the shore, often beaching themselves in their feeding frenzy. Kings of 30 to 40 pounds are mere tidbits for these mammals, which can reach lengths of over 17 feet."

Another treasure of Chuitna country lies mostly beneath its surface. The river cuts into one of the richest coal deposits in North America. Coal pieces—from small chunks to the size of small cars—line the banks of the Chuitna. Later in the year, when silver salmon enter the river, anglers will burn Chuitna coal instead of firewood to accompany their tales of fish lost and won, and to slowly simmer their foil-wrapped dinners of freshly-baked salmon. According to them, it doesn't get any better than the Chuitna.

Twelve hours after hooking his first salmon, Price was casting for kings with slowed, yet fervent energy. He had the pool to himself, and a fresh run of salmon was snaking its way up the Chuit. Watching his intense pleasure as he hooked yet another salmon made it easy to understand why anglers forsake the more popular king fisheries for the isolation and action of the Chuitna.

198

Planning Your Trip

WHEN TO GO

Mid June to the last week in July are good, with the peak of the king fishing taking place between June 15 and July 15.

WHAT TO TAKE

A 10-weight rod with plenty of spine is required for Chuitna chinooks. Take a 10-foot sink-tip line, and a full-sink line for high water, along with a supply of split shot for fast currents. Three-foot leaders with a 20-pound tippet work best for me. Bold, gaudy flies in size 2, 1 and 1/0 in Fat Freddie, Klutina king killer, copper and orange, Baker buster, Alaskabou, sparkle shrimp and saltwater herring patterns are all effective. Check regulations on fly sizes prior to heading afield.

Spin anglers use 7 1/2-foot, medium-heavy to heavy-action rods, level wind or spinning reels filled with 20-pound line, and prefer Alaskan spoons in fluorescent orange, Pixees, Mepps Aglias in chartreuse and fluorescent red, and drift lures in various fluorescent colors.

HOW TO GET THERE

Fly directly to Anchorage, with a connecting flight to Kenai. Or, you can rent a car in Anchorage and drive the Seward Highway to the Kenai Peninsula. From there, charter a flight to the Chuitna. Some air charter operators fly to the Chuit directly from Anchorage.

WHERE TO STAY

There are numerous hotels and bed and breakfasts and campgrounds in the Kenai area. Call early in the season for confirmed reservations. Several air taxi services offer overnight accommodations on the Chuitna, ranging from tent camps to cabins. Guided fishing trips are available. A full-service lodge offers rustic accommodations and meals, as well as freezer facilities.

APPROXIMATE COST

The going rate for a guided, fly-out to the Chuitna runs $200 per person. Included in the price is round-trip transportation to the Chuitna, lures and terminal tackle, and transportation to and from the river. Overnight accommodations, meals and transportation offered by lodges vary with length of stay, and start at $70 per night.

WHO TO CONTACT

For a listing of guides, outfitters and do-it-yourself services, turn to page 208, "Free Information To Plan Your Trip."

20 *Adventure*

Dollies are one of the most plentiful fish found in the Tongass National Forest. They are caught in both salt and freshwater.

Tongass Trout and Salmon on a Budget

FOR YEARS, WALT PANCHYSHYN nursed dreams of fishing Alaska. On weekends, he fished for salmon in Washington's Cowlitz River and pursued cohos and rockfish in Puget Sound. Although he enjoyed these "local" fishing trips, his heart was 1,600 miles to the north, on some unnamed Alaska stream that was loaded with fish.

"I was interested in an Alaska salmon fishing trip that offered good fishing," he said, "but didn't want to pay $3,000 a week for a lodge, or see anglers stand shoulder-to-shoulder like they do on the Russian River."

Pressure from his sons, Tony and Mike, and wife, Marlis prompted Walt and his family to make the journey to Alaska. There, they rented a cabin on Shuyak Island, and enjoyed some of the best silver salmon fishing of their lives.

Each year, Walt and many hundreds like him prove that world-class Alaska salmon and trout fishing doesn't need to cost you $4,000 a week. In many instances, you can tie into any of Alaska's five species of salmon for less than $500. In Walt's case, he spent less than $300 per person, excluding airfare.

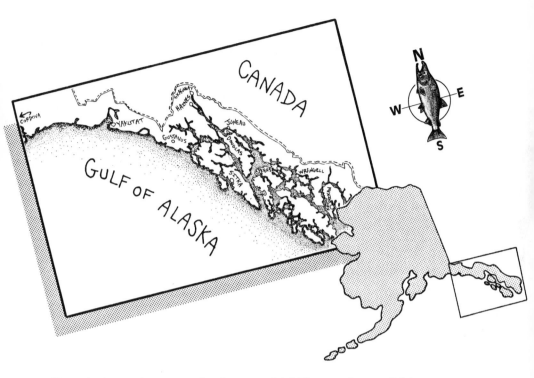

First, let's set the stage. Anglers pay $4,000 a week to a fishing lodge for *service*. Many lodges will turn back your sheets at night, provide five-course wilderness shore lunches, and even unhook your fish for you. They fly you into wilderness areas each day to fish, and cater to your every wish. You are paying for service, and the opportunity to catch a wide variety of sportfish.

But, if you're capable of catching and cleaning your own fish, cooking your own meals, and possess a basic, working knowledge of Northwest salmonids along with a burning desire for exploring new waters, then you're a prime candidate for a do-it-yourself Alaska salmon and trout adventure.

What's it going to cost you? First consider what your dollar is buying. Provided is a furnished cabin and, depending on the area, excellent fishing for sockeyes, kings, cohos, pinks, chums, trout and char, against a backdrop of fabulous mountain scenery. Many areas offer a boat for your own personal use. But wait, there's more. Chances are you'll have the stream or lake all to yourself. Would you be willing to pay $500? $800? $1,000? Close your wallet. Alaska's Tongass and Chugach national forests offer you a salmon and trout fishing extravaganza for $20 per night.

Alaska's National Forests are the sportfishing hotspots the crowds miss on their way to better-known areas. Consider that Washington, Oregon, northern California, Idaho and Michigan

For $20 per day, anglers can rent a U.S. Forest Service cabin complete with wood or oil burning stove, bunks, and on freshwater lakes and rivers, a boat for your personal use.

have a total of 15,000 miles of streams in national forests that support populations of anadromous salmon and trout. National Forests in Alaska support over 30,000 miles of streams, yet receive only 16,000 hours of angling effort annually. Yet national forests in Alaska produced over 153 million pounds of commercially caught anadromous fish in 1984. The closest runner-up was Washington and Oregon, with 7.5 million pounds.

My favorite for sportfishing action is the Tongass National Forest, which offers not only outstanding salmon fishing but also variety, with over 160 cabins from which to choose.

Tongass cabins are not run-down shacks that host beer drinking parties for the rowdies of the world. They are typically found nestled away in isolated saltwater bays near streams with one or more species of salmon. They are also located in pristine mountain passes, where cutthroat and rainbows abound, and the only company you'll see are mountain goats, brown and black bear, deer and moose.

The majority of cabins are accessible only by floatplane or extended boat travel. They house anywhere from four to seven people, and include tables, benches, wooden bunks, a wood or oil heating/cooking stove, ax, broom and outhouse. Boats are available at most cabins located on lakes.

The cabins are reserved on a first-come, first-serve basis. The north and south Situk River and Situk Weir cabins are good examples of why you need to make your reservations early. All five species of salmon are available (in season), along with some of the best steelheading in Alaska. In August, the Situk receives an excellent silver salmon run where on a good day you can catch at least 8 to 10 fish in the 10 to 15-pound range. You'll be enjoying the same fishing that others are paying over $1200 a week for. Your price? Once you arrive, $20 per day.

202

When renting a cabin, anglers are wise to bring a small cookstove, foam or air mattresses, cooking utensils and sleeping bags. Most fishing is within minutes of the cabin's front door.

The Situk cabins are popular because they are easily reached from Yakutat. In you crave isolation, other cabins to the south have equally good fishing for several species of salmon, and receive little, if any, pressure. At many cabins, you'll not see another plane, angler or person during your entire stay.

On a recent visit last August to the Pybus Bay cabin on Admiralty Island, I was astonished by the number of pink and chum salmon in the creek near our cabin. The salmon would enter the stream on an incoming tide, not in twos or threes, but in waves of 50 or more. My wife, Adela, and I spent three days fishing the stream, and didn't see another angler. In the evenings, we would explore the intertidal areas and photograph deer, eagles and brown bears. Under the thick canopy of spruce, wild berries were everywhere, and made tasty complements to salads, pancakes and oatmeal. We had found paradise, and wanted to stay an entire month.

Or, how about Sitkoh Lake cabin, a jewel of a salmon fishing get-away located on Chichagof Island near Sitka? The outlet stream is good for steelhead fishing in early spring, and supports good runs of pinks and sockeyes in mid July to August, and coho salmon in late August through September. The third week in August is a good time to catch all three species of salmon. And if salmon don't appeal to you, try the excellent cutthroat and Dolly Varden fishing in the nearby lake.

Be prepared for company on cabins located on Admiralty Island. The area has one bear per square mile. I've never been face-to-face with an Admiralty Island brownie, but you soon realize they are everywhere. Once, fishing near Mole Harbor for pinks and silvers, I spent about a half hour on the point, casting to fish. When I returned to the beach with a nice buck coho in hand, I noticed

When renting cabins in the Prince William Sound area, look carefully for glass Japanese fishing floats like the one pictured in the foreground. They are highly prized by collectors.

one of my footprints in the soft sand was obliterated by a 10-inch bear track.

When planning your trip in late fall, combine a silver salmon fishing trip with a deer hunt, all based from your Forest Service cabin. Pursue black bear, goat, wolf or grouse. It's also hard to beat a morning waterfowl hunt, followed by an afternoon of salmon fishing. The aroma of roast grouse and baked silver salmon filets at day's end will convince you it doesn't get much better than this.

My experience has been, the more remote the cabin, the better the experience. Some cabins, such as those accessible by road or trail, often receive visitors when you least expect them. This can be frustrating when you're trying to stalk up to and photograph a great blue heron standing on the bow of your boat, or taking a nap between rounds of catching salmon.

Here's a final tip: Because most of the Tongass is prime brown bear habitat, always make your presence known when traveling along streambanks and through brush. A bell or whistle works extremely well. And if a bear approaches you while you're fighting a fish, cut the line. I've yet to know of an angler who has successfully landed a 1,200-pound brown bear.

The Tongass National Forest not only offers excellent salmon fishing, but a chance to experience glaciers, wildlife, and the last great stands of wilderness forests in the United States. It's a resource that deserves to be utilized, appreciated, and respected. And at $20 per night, how can you possibly go wrong with a deal like that?

Jim Oatfield with a Situk River steelhead. The Tongass and Chugach forests have over 300 steelhead streams available. Many of the best fisheries have cabins and offer spring and/or fall runs.

Fishing Tips

Tongass National Forest streams offer a variety of fishing situations. Intertidal areas can be up to a mile or more wide, with numerous channels. Finding fish is generally no problem: just watch for bird activity; usually gulls feeding on dead salmon. Your fishing time is usually restricted to several hours before and after high tide. Low tide is also good, especially for fish holding in small pools. A word of warning: on an incoming tide, it's easy to become stranded on gravel bars in intertidal areas. Always keep tabs on the speed and intensity of an incoming tide, and give yourself plenty of time to cross the various channels to the mainland.

About several hundred yards upstream, an angler can fish without having to worry about the effects of tide on the river or stream. Here, fishing is the same as that of the Pacific Northwest: find the runs, holding pools and undercut banks, and fish accordingly. Because you'll be traveling through rain forest, plan for extra travel time. The going can be extremely difficult, with deadfalls, cliffs and other obstacles impeding progress. Walking the stream requires caution, as the bottom may be very slick with algae, especially in late July and August. I have found best success by fishing upstream at a fast pace on the first day, to discover the outlay of the stream and sample the overall fishing action. The remaining days are spent fishing the sections I like best.

Planning Your Trip

WHEN TO GO

Because of the immense size and fisheries diversity of the Tongass, listing individual anadromous runs for specific watersheds is beyond the scope of this book. Such information can be obtained through books listed below. Also, many cabins are available year-round, while others are seasonal (April through October).

WHAT TO TAKE

Pack quality raingear and warm clothing. The Tongass National Forest is located in the coastal rain forest of Southeast Alaska. Summer temperatures usually range from the mid 40s to the mid 60s, with extremes dipping into the 30s and soaring into the 80s. Annual rainfall in downtown Juneau averages 90 inches, and increases to almost 154 inches in Ketchikan.

In the Tongass, standard salmon fishing gear works best. I prefer two breakdown rods because they're easier to carry through the brush and along growth-infested riverbanks than one-piece rods. Another plus is that if one rod breaks, you can continue fishing with the spare, an important consideration when the nearest tackle store is 100 air miles away. Go with medium-action rods for kings and silvers, and lighter rods for reds, pinks and chums. A 10-weight fly rod will handle all but the most largest king salmon. Take plenty of extra line from 8 to 20-pound test. And don't forget the ultralight tackle for rainbow, cutthroat and char.

Bring your own bedding, air or foam mattress, cooking and eating utensils, flashlight, water container, toiletries, mosquito repellent, first-aid kit, 3 to 5-horse outboard motor and gasoline, portable camp stove, extra food (in case of delay in pick-up) and personal flotation devices. Be prepared to hike up to a mile or more to reach the best salmon fishing. Many of the trails are marshy, and ankle-fit hip boots offer the best protection and support. Neoprene waders are best for streams and rivers located near the cabin.

HOW TO GET THERE

From Seattle or Anchorage, take the Gold Coast Service offered by Alaska Airlines to the various cities of Southeast Alaska. Your choice of cabin will dictate whether you fly to Juneau, Ketchikan, Yakutat, Sitka, or Petersburg. From the base city, charter a boat or plane. Many cabins will be 50 minutes or less by air from the base city.

WHERE TO STAY

Permits for recreation cabins in the national forests of Alaska are issued on a first-come, first-serve basis. Permits may be obtained in person or by mail only. The current price is $20 per night, with a seven-day maximum stay.

The Tongass National Forest has over 2,000 rivers and streams that support coho salmon stocks. While most fish range from six to 12 pounds, anglers occasionally catch trophy silvers, like this 20 pounder caught by Adela Batin.

The fee goes toward maintaining cabins. Reservations may be made up to 180 days in advance.

For more information on U.S. Forest Service Cabins, obtain a copy of **"Fishing Alaska on $20 a Day,"** by Christopher and Adela Batin, a 352-page guide to inexpensively fishing the best steelhead, trout, char and salmon waters in the Tongass and Chugach forests. Profusely illustrated with over 150 maps, photographs and charts, this book provides you with hundreds of indispensable tips and information on accommodations, fish migrations, stream and lake locations as well as fish-catching advice. The book is $23.95 ppd from Alaska Angler Publications, P.O. Box 83550, Fairbanks, Alaska 99708

APPROXIMATE COSTS

Depending on type of aircraft used, expect to pay an average of $400 round-trip for transportation to the cabin. Boat charters will average about $100 an hour. Split the cost of the airfare between several people, and you can travel, from the base city, fish, and return for around $500.

WHO TO CONTACT

For a listing of guides, outfitters and do-it-yourself services, turn to page 208, "Free Information To Plan Your Trip."

Free Information For Planning Your Trip

Because the face of Alaska sportfishing is constantly changing, I have refrained from listing specific contacts at the end of each chapter. Lodges go bankrupt, guiding services deteriorate in quality, and some air charter operators compromise your safety in order to make a buck.

Part of my job as editor of *The Alaska Angler*® is to review the trends in Alaska sportfishing and each year, advise our readers accordingly. As a reader service to non-subscribers, however, you can request our free, annual guide of air charter operators, lodges, and do-it-yourself contacts necessary to fully experience the adventures in this book. These services have been selected based on positive reports from *The Alaska Angler*® subscribers and our own reviews. Services are broken down to correspond with each chapter.

For your free copy, send a self-addressed, stamped No. 10 envelope (9 3/8" x 4") to:

Alaska Angler Publications
Report No. 20
P. O. Box 83550
Fairbanks, Alaska 99708

Why this annual report?

Today's angler is bombarded with advertising hype. Many unscrupulous operators use the almost magical words, "Alaska sportfishing" to attract anglers to their fly-by-night operations. Many anglers don't know what to expect. They are pleased with their catch of three humpies or two spawned out dog salmon, when in actuality, if they had done their homework, they could have caught both large numbers and variety of ocean-fresh fish in a day's time. Our motto says it all: "Knowledge Means Success in Alaska Angling." With this free list, you receive additional, up-to-date knowledge that helps ensure your success.

An Alaska fishing trip requires careful planning and tackle selection. Each area poses diffrent fishing conditions, requiring anglers to match their fly, spin or casting tackle accordingly.

Below: When choosing clothing for fishing Alaska, stick with Thermax underwear and socks, Gore-tex socks when wearing hip boots and waders, synthetic fill vests/coats and either a Kool-Dri or Gore-tex rainsuit. Also include a camera, with film for both low and bright light conditions, and backup reels.

Epilogue

The friendship that we've established from sharing the adventures in this book doesn't have to end here. Write me about your Alaska fishing experiences, the things you've discovered, the sights you have seen and the fish you have caught.

Because no one person—myself included—knows all there is to know about Alaska sportfishing, I'm always eager to learn about new techniques, theories and successes that you've discovered, either on your own or with the help of my

fishing books and periodicals. Nothing would please me more than to hear about them directly from you, the reader of this book and my friend in Alaska sportfishing.

Let us share this common bond in an uncommon land. Write to me at P. O. Box 83550, Fairbanks, Alaska 99708.

Until then, Good Fishing.
Christopher Batin

About the Author

Over the last decade, Christopher Batin has emerged as one of Alaska's most well-known and influential sportfishing writers. He is the author of the best-selling, *"How to catch Alaska's Trophy Sportfish"* as well as *"Fishing Alaska on $15 a Day,"* *"Hunting in Alaska: A Comprehensive Guide"* and is co-author or contributor to three other books. He is editor-in-chief of *The Alaska Angler®*, a publication that provides a comprehensive look at current research in Alaska sportfishing techniques, lodge and guide reviews, do-it-yourself fishing opportunities and "inside information" on Alaska sportfishing.

He also serves as Alaska Editor for four national and regional publications which include *Western Outdoors* magazine and *Pacific Northwest Outdoors.* He has written nearly 1,000 articles and columns, many having appeared in Alaska's largest newspapers and magazines as well as *Sports Afield, In-Fisherman, Western's World, Trout, Alaska Airlines* magazine, *Saltwater Sportsman, Petersen's Fishing* and many others.

Along with his wife/fishing partner, Adela, the couple have enjoyed widespread nationwide exposure for their work in promoting Alaska sportfishing. In the last 10 years, they have appeared on the covers of 21 national and regional publications and have received recognition in numerous articles, radio talk shows and tv appearances.

Chris' dedication to producing quality work has won him over 40 national and regional writing and photography awards. These include several first-place awards for his book, *"How to catch Alaska's Trophy Sportfish,"* considered by many to be the bible on how to fish Alaska. *Field and Stream* magazine reviewed it as "Alaska Fishing Book Unparalleled." He is also the recipient of 32 trophy fish certificates sponsored by various state and national organizations.

Far from being an "arm-chair outdoor writer," Chris spends from 150 to 180 days per year traveling throughout Alaska. Much of that time is spent personally researching various tips and techniques that help anglers catch more fish. He has hiked into volcanoes, rafted glacial rivers, climbed wilderness mountains and survived Alaska's worst weather to search out and experience the state's unique, undiscovered as well as most popular sportfishing opportunities. Chris and Adela's photo file, which contains over 30,000 Alaska sportfishing transparencies, is a testimonial to this continuous quest.

Six years ago, the International Gamefish Association appointed Chris to be their Alaska representative, a title he still holds to this

Author Christopher Batin with a rainbow trout caught in the Talkeetna Mountains.

date. He helps promote the conservation goals of the organization and assists in verifying world-record fish.

When he isn't fishing some remote area of Alaska, he is in great demand for seminars and instructional classes. He is now entering his 11th year of teaching the extremely popular "Advanced Alaska Fishing Techniques™," an intense, eight-week seminar designed to help anglers increase their skills in Alaska sportfishing. Since 1984, he has been a featured seminar speaker at the Great Alaska Sportsman Show, where hundreds of people fill the bleachers to hear his dynamic presentations.

His fishing experience extends beyond Alaska. He has fished throughout Canada and the Lower 48, Mexico, Sweden, Germany, Hawaii, Japan and Russia. He says he has yet to find a place that offers the variety and quality of sportfishing that Alaska offers.

While he fly fishes for personal enjoyment and research, Chris frequently uses other types of gear to "learn whatever is necessary to increase my knowledge about fish and fishing, and pass this information on to my readers." He is equally adept at catching lunker halibut on deep-sea rigs as he is bottom-bouncing drift lures for salmon or dancing mini-jigs on a five-foot ultralight for lake trout. He is a strong advocate of catch and release, which he practices on all freshwater and anadromous fish unless they are mortally wounded. He always tries to keep a few sockeye salmon for his annual 40-below barbecue in mid December, weather and grill permitting.

Chris lives on a five-acre homesite outside Fairbanks, Alaska with wife/fishing partner Adela, dog Tiger Lily and yellow-naped Amazon parrot, Juliet. The couple is always interested in hearing about their readers' fishing adventures in Alaska.

"a publication for anglers who want the very best in Alaska sportfishing."

Dear Alaska Angling Enthusiast in Search of Adventure:

If you're planning a trip to Alaska this year, be careful.

Alaska sportfishing is not what it used to be.

In 1991, you stand a 60 percent chance of fishing with an incompetent guide.

A 35 percent chance of fishing on streams with few or no fish.

Perhaps you'll choose one of the state's unsafe air taxi operators, or one of the fishing businesses in 1990 that "left town" with the entire season's deposits from clients...businesses that are big advertisers in major magazines.

You can take your chances with the 320,000 other people who fish Alaska, and settle for mediocre catches of sportfish, or none at all.

Or you can subscribe to The Alaska Angler ®, where I will be your personal guide to Alaska's best fishing... away from the crowds.

Just ask Rick Sanchez. He had been to Alaska twice. Each time, fishing was poor, despite what the guides promised. With information he obtained from **The Alaska Angler** ®, he decided to make one last trip and fish our recommended stream where he could catch a king salmon on a fly.

A week later, Sanchez had caught 76 king salmon on flies, most from 30 to 60 pounds and set 16 world line-class records in the process. And he didn't see another angler the entire time.

Like Rick Sanchez, you, too, can benefit from **The Alaska Angler** ®. You'll know exactly what to expect before spending hundreds of dollars on a mediocre lodge or poorly-arranged do-it-yourself trip.

Make your next trip a success with information offered in **The Alaska Angler** ®.

Christopher Batin, *Editor*

Not Available in Stores!

Fishing Alaska on $15 a Day

A Comprehensive Guide to Fishing & Hunting in Alaska's National Forests

by Christopher and Adela Batin

In 1991, a seven-day stay at a premier Alaska fishing lodge will cost over $4,000, a price beyond the financial reach of many anglers.

However, if you can row a boat, cook your own meals and handle cast-after-cast excitement for feisty, fresh-from-the-sea salmon, you can enjoy comparable Alaska sport-fishing for only $15 a day. **Fishing Alaska on $15 a Day** reveals Alaska's best angling hideaways where you can catch trophy steelhead, salmon and trout. The book is the result of years of research and travel to some of Alaska's best fishing hotspots.

All the information you need for planning your trip is in this one book, saving you hundreds of dollars in research time and phone calls.

This 352-page book provides you with:

■ **Specific details on nearly 200 wilderness cabins,** exact locations, how to get there, free boats for your personal use, free cabins and shelters, and where you'll find the best wilderness sightseeing, wildlife photography and adventuring opportunities, as well as pages of alternate contact sources for more information.

■ **Available for the first time are the names and locations of over 375 Alaska steelhead streams.** Discover where you can average 8 to 12 steelhead per trip; choose from over 200 cutthroat waters, many located in Alaska's finest scenic mountain wilderness, or the best intertidal areas where fly fishermen catch over 20 silver salmon per day!

FISHING ALASKA ON $15 A DAY

A Comprehensive Guide to Fishing, Hunting & Outdoor Recreation *in Alaska's National Forests*

By Christopher and Adela Batin

ISBN 0-916771-25-3

■ **Detailed USGS topographic maps and fishing charts** help you pinpoint the best fishing and hunting areas. If purchased separately, these maps alone would cost you over $150. These maps are **FREE** with the book, and are invaluable in helping plan your trip.

■ **Specific advice on flies and lures,** as well as 100 photos to prove these recommendations work!

■ **With this book you'll also learn where you can inexpensively hunt** for moose, goat, brown and black bear, wolf and Sitka blacktail deer, as well as waterfowl. You'll have the comforts of a wilderness cabin to enjoy at the end of a successful day's hunt.

The book is profusely illustrated with over 150 maps, photographs and charts, When used in conjunction with our award-winning book, *"How to catch Alaska's Trophy Sportfish"*, you have all the information you need to plan a complete and successful Alaska fishing adventure.

"An excellent book that is essential for anyone considering making the trip."
San Francisco Examiner

"If you've dreamed about an Alaska adventure but can't afford the $2,000 to $4,000 price tag for most outfitted trips, this book is the answer."
Allentown Morning Call

"A comprehensive guide destined to become dog-eared by dedicated anglers. Written by Chris Batin, perhaps the best-known fishing authority in Alaska."
Akron Beacon

Fishing Alaska on $15 a Day.....$19.95

How to catch Alaska's Trophy Sportfish

By Christopher Batin

"Alaska Fishing Book Unparalleled" *Rich Landers Field and Stream magazine*

Over 30,000 anglers around the world have benefited from this advanced guide.

Anyone can catch four-pound rainbows or 12-pound salmon. But if you want to catch 60 to 80-pound Alaska king salmon, 300-pound halibut, 20-pound silvers, 30-inch rainbow trout, trophy grayling and steelhead, **"How to catch Alaska's Trophy Sportfish"** is your must-have, on-stream guide.

How to catch
Alaska's Trophy Sportfish
by Christopher Batin
Foreword by Homer Circle
Angling Editor of Sports Afield

ISBN 0-916771-03-2

This book is also a must-have volume to fully understand the author's fishing recommendations in "Fishing Alaska on $15 a Day."

"Batin's long time on Alaskan waters (over 30,000 hours) gives his new book singular value. What fisherman wouldn't pay for a decade of experience condensed into plain English? The author's experience shows. No matter what the species being sought, Batin's book is a great place to start." Joe Bridgman
The Anchorage Times.

This book can make your Alaska fishing trip a success with its:

■ 368 pages and 120 action-filled photos showing you the fish-catching secrets that has enabled the author to catch and release thousands of sportfish.

■ Fly fishing techniques for Alaska's lakes and streams.

■ Detailed information, life histories, and feeding habits for all of Alaska's 17 major sportfish species.

■ Over 500 specific areas in Alaska where you can catch your trophy sportfish.

■ 16 full-color pages identifying Alaska's trophy sportfish plus color charts of the most effective lure and fly patterns.

■ Detailed charts and illustrations showing you where to find trophy sportfish.

■ Fish-catching secrets of over a dozen guides and biologists.

This Book Gives You A PH.D. Crash Course In Alaska Fish Habits and Biology Necessary for Success

"How to catch Alaska's Trophy Sportfish" translates volumes of biological data into terms every angler can understand and use to catch trophy sportfish.

You'll learn about:
■ aggravation responses that catch 70-pound salmon,
■ social hierarchies that tell you where to find fish before you reach the water,
■ stream equations necessary for catching the largest trout and char.

We show you how each species of Alaska trophy sportfish respond to stimuli, and how you can duplicate those responses through our proven field tips and techniques. If you order NOW, you can have this knowledge today...at your fingertips.

Use this book when you go shopping for flies and tackle.

You receive sixteen full-color pages showing the different sportfish and the best flies and lures you need for success, all of which have earned the highest marks for catching trophy sportfish in 10 years of testing.

With this advice, you'll spend your time catching fish, rather than wondering what to catch them on.

"If you plan to go to Alaska, or already live there, read this book thoroughly and you fish it better. Chris Batin IS Alaska fishing."
Homer Circle
Angling Editor, Sports Afield magazine

How to catch Alaska's Trophy Sportfish
Softcover $24.95
Hardcover-Limited Edition...........$45.

The Alaska Hunter®

Dear Alaska Hunter:

Before you make another Alaska big game hunt, heed this warning: **The hunting crowds are getting worse.**

...In many areas, game animals are not as large as they used to be.

The market is flooded with incompetent guides out to make a quick buck.

Statistics show that guides typically harvest 8-foot bears because they lack the skill and knowledge to find larger bears for their clients.

And do-it-yourself hunters who don't have an insider providing them with Alaska hunting information seldom enjoy the areas they are in, or the fruits of a successful hunt...

However, now YOU can regularly receive the inside scoop on:

■ Where the largest big game animals are taken,

■ The undiscovered, do-it-yourself trips that offer near 100 percent success rates;

■ The guides with high success rates for big bears, trophy moose and caribou.

These successful hunters all have one thing in common. They subscribe to **The Alaska Hunter®**

With **The Alaska Hunter®** as your guide, you become one of the state's most knowledgeable hunters. Why? Because with each issue, you receive the most current reports and analyses necessary for success.

You can look elsewhere for this information, but don't expect to find it. Conventional sources of information offer you fluffy stories with no substance. Rarely do these stories satisfy the informational needs of knowledgeable hunters who demand specifics such as harvest figures, game densities, access corridors, and information on guides and outfitters offering outstanding trips, or do-it-yourself hunts with high success ratios.

The Alaska Hunter provides you with all this information...and more.

We cater to you, the experienced hunter who wants the very best. And with **The Alaska Hunter®** , you receive specific answers to your Alaska big game hunting questions.

In each issue, you can expect...

At least a dozen new contacts necessary for a successful Alaska hunting trip...outfitters, guides, air charter operators, biologists, hunting experts. Save valuable time and money by allowing us to do the legwork for you. Just the contacts and references you receive each month are worth the yearly subscription price in money saved from expensive long-distance phone calls!

With **The Alaska Hunter®** , you receive the facts without bias from booking agents, bribed writers or advertisements.

Our only allegiance is to you.

We receive no commissions for the trips or contacts we report. No gun reporting or adventure stories. Only unbiased objective reports on Alaska hunting. You won't find this information anywhere else. Pure and simple.

In each bi-monthly issue, you receive specific answers to your Alaska big game hunting questions. You'll receive:

Do-It-Yourself Alaska Hunter
A special page with complete where-to, how-to information on planning your Alaska big game hunt, by yourself or with a group. Prices, logistics, transportation, chances of success, special equipment, game populations, best ways to ship home trophies and meat, companies that rent float hunting gear.

Hunt Reviews
The best and worst do-it-yourself and guided hunts for every species of Alaska big game. In future issues, discover Alaska's best trophy moose area, where record-book bulls are dying of old age...read where the current, world-record brown bear is living, and why hunters haven't been able to bag him...how two-plane hunts offer 80 to 100 percent success ratios...the story behind the rip-off $400 fly-out hunt special, and more.

Hunt Area Specifics
In-depth reports on a specific game management units, what's available, type of terrain, weather, success figures for each species of big game animals, and more. This is information that would take you weeks to acquire on your own.

The Best of the Best
Alaska hunting guides and outfitters who are providing the very best guided trophy and do-it-yourself hunts. In-depth profiles on the guides whose clients are regulars in the Boone and Crockett, Pope and Young and Safari Club record books.

Secrets of Alaska's Hunting Guides
Tips gleaned from veteran guides with decades of field experience. Their observations and tips can spell the difference between success and failure.

Alaska Hunter News Updates
The most current news of the Alaska hunting industry, disciplinary actions, outfitter problems, USFWS sting operations on registered guides and renegade outfitters, new hunt openings, hunt closures, and Department of Fish and Game management decisions.

Marine Mammal Coverage
Ready for walrus, seal or polar bearhunting? The Alaska Hunter will keep you up-to-date on the status of

the Marine Mammal Protection Act, and who the top guides will be so you'll be ready when the seasons open.

Guide/Outfitter Issues
The inside stories behind the guides' push for dominance in the hunting market. How Alaska's big game populations are in trouble from unregulated hunting by renegade outfitters. The detrimental effect some air taxi operators are having on your hunting success.

Political Forum
Up-to-date reports on important political decisions and actions that affect you and your Alaska hunting plans. This is especially important as Alaska moves toward deregulation of guide areas, Native Sovereignty, 1991 amendments, and removal of prime hunting lands by the National Park Service.

Discounts
■ Last minute hunt cancellations
■ Special hunt openings
■ The best registration hunts
■ Waterfowl/big game hunts
■ Fishing/hunting combos and more

The information you'll receive each month is an unbeatable combination of experience and knowledge.

It's created for hunters like you by year-long resident Alaska hunters and writers. And they are directed by Chris Batin, one of Alaska's most experienced hunting writers and editors.

Batin is author of the award-winning, "Hunting in Alaska: A Comprehensive Guide," and former editor of Alaska Outdoors magazine and The Alaska Professional Hunter newsletter. He has received over 30 awards for his reports in national and regional publications, including the Journalist of the Year from the Alaska Professional Hunters

Association and Sportswriter of the Year from The Alaska Outdoor Council. With over 15 years of experience covering the Alaska hunting scene, Chris is both as an active participant and veteran journalist. He is considered by many of the country's top outdoor writers as one of Alaska's most knowledgeable hunting editors.

Compare us with other publications on the market. A year's subscription is only **$49**, which includes first-class postage to your home or office.

If you want the very best of Alaska big game hunting, you can't afford to be without a subscription to The Alaska Hunter.

Don't miss a single issue. Send in the attached order form or call toll free today and be among those who benefit from **The Alaska Hunter**®

The Alaska Hunter.........$49 per year.

Hunting in Alaska
A Comprehensive Guide

By Christopher Batin

''(Hunting in Alaska) is the standard by which other Alaska hunting books will be judged.''
Bob Robb,
Petersen's Hunting

Hunting in Alaska is a rich source of Alaska-tested hunting ideas & strategies that work!
■ 416 information-packed pages, 138 photos, many award winning
■ 51 maps & illustrations
■ Expert advice on hunting sheep, bear, moose, caribou, waterfowl, and more!
■ Detailed, where-to-go information and harvest statistics for each species in each Game Management Unit

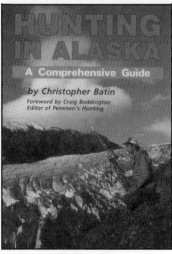

ISBN 0-916771-02-4

■ Detailed maps and Game Management Unit descriptions that will familiarize you with Alaska's wilderness hunting hotspots and game concentrations.
■ Planning a do-it-yourself hunt.
■ Secret bear hunting techniques used by one guide who is nearly 100 percent for big brown bear, and who has put several in the record books, including a 30-incher.
■ Criteria for choosing an Alaska big game guide.
■ Learn secrets of taking wolves along salmon streams

For years, successful guides and hunters have known that it takes scientific knowledge and specific strategies to successfully harvest Alaska's most coveted big game trophies.

Now, for the first time, **Hunting in Alaska: A Comprehensive Guide** offers you over 1,000 of these hunting secrets and tips. Master guides and big game experts provide decades of first-hand experience, ensuring your Alaska hunt is a complete success.

Based on 15 years of Alaska hunting experience and research, ''Hunting in Alaska: A Comprehensive Guide'' **provides you with a wealth of never-before available information on:**
■ High Bush and Low Bush Thrashing: Tactics scientifically proven to call in trophy moose.
■ Specifics on hunting Kodiak and Alaska Peninsula Brown Bear
■ Scientific data on the habits of full-curl Dall sheep, where they're found and how to hunt them, including interviews with guides who regularly take record-book sheep.
■ 10-year trends on game populations, hunter statistics and harvest totals that give you pre-hunt knowledge of your chances for success in each of Alaska's 26 Game Management Units.

■ Understanding seasonal migration habits of big mountain goats and goat hunting methods that have helped one guide bag over 40 trophy goats for his clients.
■ Specialized equipment needs for guided, unguided, backpack and float hunts.
■ Over 1,000 listings of where you can hunt Alaska's big and small game and waterfowl.
■ Care of trophies and meat.
■ How to hunt ridges, over bait, berry patches, and tidal flats for trophy black bear.
■ Extensive chapters on duck, goose, sea duck and crane hunting, small game, grouse, ptarmigan.
■ Four award-winning stories on Alaska Hunting Excitement, Ethics, Camaraderie, and Adventure.
■ Big game behavioral and natural history information of special interest to you as a hunter. Historical synopses of Alaska big game species, including transplants and current distribution information.

Hunting in Alaska: A Comprehensive Guide

Softcover $24.95
Hardcover $34.95

Bear Heads & Fish Tales

By Alan Liere

Patrick F. McManus, internationally recognized humorist, book author and columnist for Outdoor Life magazine, has this to say in the foreword of Alan Liere's recent book on Alaska outdoor humor entitled, "**Bear Heads & Fish Tales**":

"What's funny? Nobody knows for sure, but I would venture to say that it's that tiny, gritty bit of truth that produces the pearl of laughter. I do not mean to imply that author Al Liere in any way resembles an oyster. The man is a funny writer, which is the best thing you can say about a humorist. I personally plan to buy a gross of Bear Heads & Fish Tales. If we have another Great Depression, people will need something to cheer them up, and I figure a copy of this book will be as good as gold in the marketplace."

Bear Heads & Fish Tales is a collection of zany outdoor stories written by Alan Liere, Alaska's ambassador of mirth and humor to the funny bone. Learn the techniques for smoking fish, Alaska-style, by burning your neighbors garage; what words to say to your oil pan while sleeping under your car, tips on preparing wilderness gourmet meals such as Chicken Noodle Salmon or 'Humpy Rainwater Soup, how to stuff a mature bull caribou into the cargo space of a Subaru hatchback and much more.

"This book is for anyone who has ever wielded a fishing rod, a shotgun, or a wiener stick," says Liere. "It's for those who experience deflated air mattresses, rubber rafts, and egos— sometimes all on the same outing. **Bear Heads & Fish Tales** is for anyone who believes in that fine line between tragedy and comedy and knows with all their heart that maturity is highly over-rated."

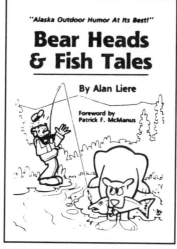

"Alaska Outdoor Humor At Its Best!"

Bear Heads & Fish Tales

By Alan Liere

Foreword by
Patrick F. McManus

ISBN 0-916771-05-9

The 13 stories in this 139-page book are based on Liere's real-life personal misadventures and hilarious insights. In "King Tut's Revenge," Liere expounds on his childhood phobia regarding mummy-type sleeping bags. "Thanks, Aunt Judy" reveals tips on how Liere has learned to survive Alaska mosquitoes through such evasive tactics as "The Screamin' Exit" and the liberal use of garlic. And with a humorous eye, he examines that glossy, hope-inducing product of creative writing and adjective overuse known as "The Alaska Outdoor Brochure."

Each story is illustrated by outdoor cartoonist Jeff Schuler. The combined efforts of both author and cartoonist effectively capture the side-splitting antics and foibles of sportsmen in the Alaska outdoors, the Northcountry's grandest comic playhouse.

Bear Heads & Fish Tales $9.95

©1991 Batin Communications Network, Inc.

Alaska Angler® Information Service

Want to know the best rivers to catch all five species of Pacific salmon? Anxious to discover the Top 10 do-it-yourself trips for wild, 8 to 10-pound rainbow trout? Or a listing of Alaska's five-star lodges that serve you early-morning coffee in bed and at night, place European chocolates on your pillow?

The answers to these and other Alaska sportfishing questions can be answered by dialing a toll-free number and asking for the **Alaska Angler Information Service**.

The Information Service provides "answers for anglers" who are planning a fishing trip to the 49th state.

"There's a common misconception that Alaska fishing is good year-round, no matter where or when you go," says Chris Batin, editor of **The Alaska Angler**® . "Alaska has over 3 million lakes and 3,000 rivers covering a land mass one-fifth the size of the continental United States. Planning is crucial for success. A miscalculation of several days can have anglers staring at fishless water rather than a stream filled with salmon."

He stressed the information service is not a booking agency.

"Objectivity is the key to the Alaska Angler Information Service," Batin said. "We do not receive any remuneration or benefit from recommending one stream or fishing service over another. This ensures that our customers receive objective information on fishing opportunities, guides and lodges that surpass industry standards for service, quality and professionalism. We can provide all the information anglers need, from the best flies for a particular watershed, water conditions to expect, type of hatches, and even the flora and fauna in the area."

Travel agents and booking agents are often unfamiliar with Alaska's myriad sportfishing options.

"Many travel agents sell a limited selection of trips that offer the best commissions for them," he said. "It's not cost effective for them to recommend quality, inexpensive trips, even though it may be perfect for the angler's needs. The Alaska Angler Information Service provides unbiased information so the angler can personally decide whether to spend $25 or $4,000 for a trip.

The crew of **The Alaska Angler** spends over 180 days a year fishing Alaska, searching out the best do-it-yourself and full-service adventures for the company's information service, periodicals and books.

The cost is $25 for 15 minutes of consultation. Before consultation begins, callers provide a Mastercard or Visa credit card number. To expedite matters, have ready your list of questions. To benefit from the Alaska Angler Information Service, call **1-800-446-2286** 10 a.m. to 6 p.m. Alaska Standard Time, Mon.—Fri. To set up an appointment call (907) 456-8212.

Ship to:_____

Address:_____

City _____

State_____ Zip_____

Daytime Phone(   )_____

Send order to:

Alaska Angler® Publications
P.O. Box 83550
Fairbanks, Alaska 99708
(907) 456-8212

Or Call TOLL FREE 1-800-446-2286
Mon.—Fri., 10 a.m.—6 p.m. Alaska Standard Time

Quantity	Item	Price	Total
_____	Chris Batin's 20 Great Alaska Fishing Adventures.........................	$19.95	_____
_____	Fishing Alaska on $15 a Day..	$19.95	_____
_____	How to catch Alaska's Trophy Sportfish, softcover........................	$24.95	_____
_____	How to catch Alaska's Trophy Sportfish, Limited Edition, hardcover.......	$45.	_____
_____	Hunting in Alaska, softcover, ...	$24.95	_____
_____	Hunting in Alaska, hardcover, ...	$34.95	_____
_____	Bear Heads and Fish Tales..	$9.95	_____
_____	The Alaska Angler® (one-year subscription)............................	$49. ppd	_____
_____	The Alaska Hunter® (one-year subscription).............................	$49. ppd	_____
_____	The Alaska Angler® Custom Binder.......................................	$14. ppd	_____
_____	The Alaska Hunter® Custom Binder.......................................	$14. ppd	_____
_____	Back issues of The Alaska Angler®	$8.50 each ppd	_____
	___ , ___ , ___ , ___ , ___ , ___ , ___ , ___ , ___	3 for $21. ppd	_____
_____	Back issues of The Alaska Hunter®	$8.50 each ppd	_____
	___ , ___ , ___ , ___ , ___ , ___ , ___ , ___ , ___	3 for $21. ppd	_____
_____	"Alaska Angler® " poplin leisure cap, one size fits all..................	$14. ppd	_____
	Circle color: Teal Green Red		
_____	"Alaska Angler® " leisure cap, one size fits all..........................	$17. ppd	_____
	Circle color and fabric: Teal Green Red Corduroy Ripstop Nylon		
_____	"Alaska Angler" Polo shirt, Circle size and color....................	$38.50 ppd	_____
	Teal Green Red Orchid Men's sizes: S M L XL		

Gift Section

Book(s) personalized to: (please print)

Name _____

Title of book(s) _____

_____

Book(s) personalized to:

Name _____

Title of book(s) _____

_____

Book(s) personalized to:

Name _____

Title of book(s) _____

_____

Book Shipping Charges

Priority Mail delivery (1 to 2 weeks)......$6. _____
each additional book Priority Mail...............$3. _____
Bookrate delivery (4 to 5 weeks)............$4. _____
each additional book Bookrate...................$2. _____
Newsletters, binders, apparel postage paid....0.
Canada, add to above charges................$3. _____
Foreign countries, Airmail, per book....$15. _____
Airmail, per newsletter subscription..........$20. _____

ORDER AND SHIPPING TOTAL _____

Payment Method

Enclose your personal check, money order or credit card information.

☐ **Check**   ☐ **Money Order**   ☐ **VISA**   ☐ **Mastercard**

Card Acct. Number_____

Exp. Date   —   Signature _____